Single.

Women.

Entrepreneurs.

By Erin Albert

IBJ Book Publishing
a division of IBJ Media
41 E. Washington St., Suite 200
Indianapolis, IN 46204
www.ibjbp.com
(317) 634-6200

First Edition

ISBN: 978-1-934922-40-8

Library of Congress Control Number: 2011920397

Printed in the United States of America
La Vergne, Tennessee

To all the bold, daring, single, and smart women in the universe.

Table of Contents

The Single. Women. Entrepreneurs.

Acknowledgements

I would be remiss if I didn't put the acknowledgements in the very front of this particular book project, simply because there is no way this project would have been completed without the following people in my life connecting, supporting and helping me grow this amazing collection of fantastic women. To the following, I want to sincerely thank you for helping me bring this project to life!

In particular, I would like to thank one of my mentors, Billie Dragoo, for connecting me to Lorin Beller-Blake of Big Fish Nation, who connected me to a LOT of the amazing women in this book. Thank you! Also, thank you to the following people, who connected me to others for this project as well: Kathleen McDonald, Keith Crawford, Claudia Brink, Denise Bonk, Sarah Sladek, Jen Dalton, Mandy Dalton, Vern Ludden, and Jerry Bonnet. Also, to my mom and sounding board, Dorothy Albert, thanks for reading and helping with this project. Also, to the guardian of all my crazy ideas, Chris Russell, I thank you. Also, to Dr. Elaine Voci, thank you as always for reminding me that writing a book is not a project, but a journey.

Last but certainly not least, I'd like to thank my publishers at IBJ Media: Mickey Maurer, Pat Keiffner, Jodi Belcher, and Scott Swain. Of course, thanks to all the amazing women in this book— thank you for the inspiration! As well, thanks to all the women who considered being part of this book, and of course, to my fearless leaders at Butler University who always support my research and ideas: Dr. Julie Koehler and Dean Mary Andritz.

Thank you to all!!!

Introduction

On January 28, 1813, the now world famous book, *Pride and Prejudice*, was officially published by Jane Austen. It is one of my favorite books. In her book, she states the following: "It is a truth universally acknowledged, that a single man in possession of a good fortune, must be in want of a wife." Nearly 200 years later, and very close to the same publishing date of Ms. Austen, I'm going to submit to you, the reader, the following quote in this book: It is a truth universally acknowledged, that a single woman in possession of a good fortune (or not), must be in want of … an enterprise. Perhaps it is not yet a universal truth, but I believe, after interviewing many single women entrepreneurs, that it is on its way to being true. I'm in hopes this book helps bring the idea of a universal truth closer to reality.

I promised myself I wouldn't start my sixth book until I got back to the United States. But, it just sounds so much cooler to share with you that I'm sitting on a patio in a hotel in Beijing, China, writing to you my very first lines of a project that I hope will be a tremendous asset to the future of something I'm personally passionate about: entrepreneurship. It's true! I really am in China, spending four weeks trying to understand how the law of China works, and comparatively—how law is similar and different between China and the United States.

Honestly, this study (a summer law program, of all things) lit the fire to start this book early for me. China is a developing country, and they are slowly but surely learning how to dominate the global business world. After seeing and appreciating how they live and work (the minimum wage here is around $1 an hour, and the college students get up at 6 a.m. each day to practice their English), I have to say, now is the best time ever for women who want to start a business not only in the U.S., but perhaps anywhere in the world. In China, they are eager and willing to work hard to become a super power. Are we as a country in the U.S.? I certainly hope so. We live in the greatest country on the planet, particularly for the innovative, creative, and entrepreneurial.

So you might be thinking, OK, I get it, but why are you only studying *single* women business owners? Well, that all comes back to home. I am divorced, and fell into my first business as the 'accidental entrepreneur' in 2005 as a single, and my second business a year later. As I've written in previous books, I had absolutely no idea what I was doing then, and honestly still don't know if I fully understand what it is that I'm doing with my businesses now. However, I'm having a blast trying to figure things out! One of my current businesses (Yuspie, LLC) focuses primarily on the young urban single professional. Everywhere I look, there are single professionals paving their own way through life, but in my opinion, there is not enough support for their plight in the media, in books, and on television.

This, coupled with all the buzz about the lack of innovation in the world (be it back home in Indianapolis, Indiana, or even here in Beijing, China), and the report recently published by the Kauffman Foundation (a think tank that studies entrepreneurship) on gender and entrepreneurship, I was struck by a particular chart in the report, which (finally) explored the differences between men and women entrepreneurs. This table (Table 2, if you want to look it up, here: www.kauffman.org/uploadedFiles/successful_women_entrepreneurs_5-10.pdf) I found fascinating. It basically showed that more single, widowed, divorced and never married women than men started businesses. As I rifled through the text to find an explanation as to why, I frustratingly never found one.

That is the genesis of this book. I'm curious to know why more solo women than men start businesses. Also, are they having more success? Different success? What *is* success to a single woman business owner? Do they have some advantages that married women or men don't have starting a business? Naturally, I did the token Amazon search on the topic and surprise—didn't find anything there either. (Lesson learned: if you amazon.com search a book idea and can't find it, it is your job to write it. My five other books utilized the same topic identification process, and I recently learned that Toni Morrison agrees with this notion of writing.)

So here I am, on a patio, in the northwest side of Beijing, China, drinking (imported) Budweiser, writing this intro as to why I'm taking on this project. In the end, here are my hypotheses (you can read the book and check me, but I'm not changing my mind until the end of my research):

1. Single people start more businesses because they *have* to. Multiple streams of income are the future. The new "safe" is to have multiple streams of income simultaneously.

2. Married people usually have a plan B: a spouse that can take care of them, when the fit hits the shan. Singles don't have that. Therefore, singles must learn how to create their own individual plan Bs. A business can be a primary or secondary income stream.

3. Singles have some hidden advantages that may be exposed for the first time ever in this book. I'll save what I think they are to see if they come through the interviews.

4. With those advantages, singles also have some disadvantages to owning a business. What are they, and do they actually lead to a detrimental effect on the success of the business? I think they might actually be advantages in some ways instead of disadvantages …

5. How does owning a business as a singleton affect one's personal life? Does it actually lead to marriage, or are personal status and business status totally separate and independent factors from each other? My guess is that

more singles actually marry after they start and establish their businesses than not.

6. People are living longer. People are also waiting to get married. This means more time solo. But the average person starting a business—are they older or younger than the average person with marriage on the mind? I don't know.

7. What about social businesses, like low profit limited liability companies (L3Cs) and Benefit Corporations? What do women think about these forms of business, and do they fit the rationale for why single women are starting businesses?

It is also important to share with you what this book is NOT. If you want to learn more on how to start a business, there are PLENTY of books already out there on that topic. Furthermore, the following 30 interviews were conversations with single women business owners; therefore, the tone of the book is also conversational. (Grammar police: you've officially been warned.) I really wanted to stay as true to the tone of each entrepreneur as humanly possible.

My writing mentor always told me that writing a book is not a process, but instead a journey. After interviewing all thirty plus women (I did interview more than 30, but I have included 30 interviews in this book), I've concluded at the end of the book some things I learned as common 'themes' from these single women and their motives to start a business. I can't wait to find out more about these fascinating women: the single women entrepreneurs!

The Single. Women. Entrepreneurs.

Kathryn Alexander, MA

Ethical Impact, L3C

Kathryn Alexander, *president & CEO of Ethical Impact, L3C is a serial entrepreneur & author of the forthcoming book,* Ethics of Sustainability. *The creator of the Sustainable Values Set®, providing education on sustainability issues, and certifying sustainable businesses using the Forever Green™ certification process, she helps leaders and teams create and navigate their desired future. In her 16 years working with change in organizations ranging from start-ups to Fortune 50 companies, she has learned the secret that effective organizations are ethical organizations. Working with leaders and teams to think differently about their problems, she has been instrumental in co-creating significant shifts in her client companies. The alignment of a company from strategy to customer is a robust approach to long-term effectiveness, and integral to Kathryn's approach. Her passion is developing leadership that generates enlightened business practices to create effective and sustainable business communities.*

Her client list includes the Department of Public Works—City and County of San Francisco, Union Carbide, U.S. Army Corps of Engineers, Pacific Telesis, Mervyn's, AT&T, and Rochester Telephone. Kathryn developed the Birds of a Feather™ model, a tool for strategically assessing organizational culture, the Strategic Values Set® model assessment, and with Verna Allee is the co-author of the Quality Tools Matrix™.

***Ethical Impact L3C** is a social benefit company that supports companies implementing strategic sustainable business practices through consulting, education, auditing and certification. They love life, the planet and people. Their joy is seeing their clients grab hold of their vision, join hands with Mother Nature and make a difference in the world. The company can be reached at www.ethicalimpact.com, by email at ka@ethicalimpact.com and by phone at (888) 331-7492.*

Can you describe your business in one sentence?

We are a consulting, auditing, and certification company, bringing companies to life by bringing the value of strategic sustainability to organizations.

Why did you start Ethical Impact, L3C, and how long has it been around?

I have spent years working with executives in a consulting capacity and learned from that how important leadership is, and how important values are in how leaders act. I developed proprietary tools to help leaders understand their own personal values and help them understand how those values actually control how they work versus how they think they are working. Originally, the business came into being in 2003 as a corporation. Then in 2009, I decided to make it a limited liability company (LLC), largely because I had been sick for 5 years. I had liver cancer, a punctured colon and had 2 hips replaced. When I returned to work in 2009, I made it a LLC. Then in 2010, I discovered the L3C and reincorporated it as a L3C.

By Erin Albert

Ethical Impact is a low profit limited liability company, or a L3C, which is a business form currently available in about 10 states in the U.S. What is a L3C, how is it different from traditional business models, like a LLC, and why did you choose a L3C as your preferred business model?

Here is how I describe a L3C: A for profit business is like a car with profit in the driver's seat. A not for profit business is like a car with mission in the driver's seat. A L3C is like a car with mission in the front seat, and profit in the back seat. I felt that the L3C business entity type or model created more alignment between the values I espoused and the changes I was trying to make in business.

You personally believe that a business has an obligation not only to make a profit, but also be "sustainable." What does that term mean to you?

Sustainability to me means that a business is going to be around for a long time. The earth has been here for 3.8 billion years and humans have been on it for about 5 million years. I have yet to meet anyone who believes that if we keep on doing what we're doing we'll be here for another 1,000 years. Can we really manage being on the planet for another 5 million years doing the same things we've been doing? No.

The standard definition of sustainability is meeting our current needs without sacrificing the needs of future generations. We need to preserve and regenerate what we have on this planet. If we are going to continue to be here, we have to find ways to sustain business and not destroy the planet and allow it to re-establish itself. The prime directive of the planet is to create the conditions that support life; should we do less? In the long term, that's what we also have to do. But we don't do that. We create conditions that make life impossible over the long term.

How do businesses, then, get back to sustainability?

The really simple answer is that we make work that not just allows us to be alive, but to be alive with JOY. We TOLERATE our work in a lot of cases, thinking things are going to change in the future. But a lot of people really don't live their lives with joy nor love what they do. We have to begin with the end in mind. I think this has been one of the blessings with entrepreneurship, in that people who are entrepreneurs get the opportunity to create a life that they love. While they all don't necessarily arrive there, they have the control to potentially create the life they want to live.

Ethical Impact also has a B Corp certification. What is B Corp certification, and why did you obtain it for your company?*

Same reason why I moved to a L3C business structure—B Corp is working to change the law so that companies are legally required to pay as much attention to the community and their environment as they pay to their shareholders and the bottom line. Right now, you only legally have to focus on the shareholder; it's OK to destroy the environment and the community around you in order to make money. Being a B Corp demonstrates that my company is committed to being sustainable—to the environment, to the community around my business, and to profits. I've committed to the concept of sustainability for my business.

[To learn more about B Corp certification, logon to: www.bcorporation.net. It is important to note that there is a B Corp certification process, which is available nationally, and a business structure called a Benefit Corporation, which is currently available only in the states of Maryland and Vermont.]

What advantages do you think you have as a single business owner that perhaps married business owners do not have?

I think again it depends on the person. There are really two levels of entrepreneurship: 1. Providing your own job—what most small business is, and 2. Creating wealth. These two types of entrepreneurs have very different strategies to go about creating their endpoints. Most of my life, I've created my own job. I've made enough money to live. I've also enjoyed flexibility to raise my kids. Business ownership gave me the flexibility to be around for my kids while they were growing up. Now that I'm building a bigger business, I'm finding it a much more consuming process.

What about disadvantages?

You do EVERYTHING. You live and die by your own work, which I'd want to do anyway, but you're responsible for the quality of the life that you create, and you don't necessarily have the illusion of security. BUT, you can be fired at any time or let go from a day job and we've seen a lot of that lately. That leaves you with nothing AND a sense of powerlessness, because you're waiting for someone else to let you do something in order to get paid. As an entrepreneur, you have things to offer the world, so it's empowering to be able to make a difference in your life and the world by being on your own. It also allows you to be much more creative and innovative. Technically, now I'm unemployable because I'm very creative and innovative and that's not always well regarded in the corporate environment.

So, you are saying that companies pay you as a consultant to give them advice using creative and innovative skill sets, but you're unemployable because your innovative and creative as a full-time employee?

Yes. Ironic!

Do you think business ownership has led you to remain single?

No, I think if I had an interest, I could get married. But I will say that especially right now, while I'm trying to create a larger organization, it does require a lot of time and energy—and a relationship with a significant other would almost feel distracting.

What advice would you give another single woman who is thinking about starting a business?

Part of the joy we get out of life is feeling like we really contributed something. We need to go for it! I've actually spent the early years of my business life helping high school students start their own businesses. I've watched students employ their parents, and other adults offering to buy the businesses of the students I've helped. Anyone can do it! You don't need money either, just a great idea. Encouragement is what is necessary. It is something you can do with nothing.

What about being a single WOMAN business owner? Have you perceived advantages or disadvantages to being a woman business owner?

There's always a disadvantage with being a woman in business dealing with men. It's really hard for men to feel comfortable around women in the workplace, or believe that women have the same level of knowledge and authority that they do. Men and women work differently. Men are about ranking. There's a lot of ways they test and share how they're better than the other men. Women don't do that; we're much more about connection, who you know, who supported us, and that determines our ranking status. That's definitely had an impact on my effectiveness.

In terms of advantages: you have to be good at what you do and people will recognize it. But a lot of it is about salesmanship and you can sell as a woman or as a man. That's bigger than anything else. It's also hard for women sometimes to be effective in situations where they need to be really aggressive or clever. For some people in business, it is about winning at all costs. And, there are people who view business as a game. Women anticipate that the relationship will count for something, and in the game, it doesn't count for as much.

What is the business/entrepreneurial climate like for women in business in Colorado? Are there organizations that help women in business?

We are an entrepreneurial hotbed. In Colorado, there are more sustainable and organic companies that are values-based. I came from California to Colorado, and there is definitely more value-based business interest here. People here are really interested in creating a life, having fun, doing business with integrity and making the world a better place, rather than just becoming wealthy.

Honestly, I have had a hard time in the past connecting with a lot of women's business organizations. So many of them wanted to talk about fashion instead of real business information. I can get information on fashion anywhere, but I really need to know how to raise capital, how to talk to investors, etc., and I never found that. This by and large isn't a topic of interest to a lot of women I've talked to. There are a lot of women who have their own job, but it is a much different level of business when creating wealth vs. evolving in a job. It's a whole new ball game. Raising capital is a very different business skill, and I would guess that 85-90% of small businesses really don't want to grow to large levels.

What was the best training you received to prepare you as a business owner?

I don't think I really had any training. I stumbled into it and did what seemed to work. When I moved to Colorado and decided to actually create a company, not just a business, I was lucky to find CEO Space. That was the first place for me to understand the difference between having a job and creating a company. That resource has given me a lot of information and support. The Business Catapult (www.businesscatapult.com) also had a great focus and help for me on entrepreneurship. There are so many other things that happen when you have to have investment in order to create what it is that you want to do. If you're selling a product, you might need money to buy the product, or build a technology infrastructure, or create a plant to build, whatever it is that you want to make. You're going to need a lot of capital for that, and that in turn opens up a whole other world of possibilities—and learning. You're talking to investors at other levels and you need to know how to legally ask for money. It is entirely a new learning curve.

Did you, or are you running your business as a part-time or full-time venture? Why?

Single. Women. Entrepreneurs.

It always FELT like full-time! But I am a serial entrepreneur. I even had a business when my kids were growing up—a cleaning service. I could and did help clients all day long, as long as I had control over my own schedule. I was able to manage the work without feeling that I had to be somewhere from 9-5. Even now, a lot of the work I do doesn't happen during 9-5. I have a lot of appointments or meetings during that timeframe, but a lot of my work happens early in the morning or late at night. So, it has allowed me to have a life but I've never been constrained by the 9-5 work day. I can take breaks when I need to take them. The one exception to that of course is when you have a retail store. I had one of the first weaving and spinning stores in the country during the 1970s.

Were your parents entrepreneurs?

No. My mom was a teacher and dad was a chemist.

Did you take on a partner in your business at any time?

No. Although at this point in time, starting this year, I have been working with a group of people collaboratively and we are thinking of creating a consortium in a more formal way. I've had employees but never had a partner. I'm hoping someone will step up in the future, but no one has yet.

If you had to start another business, what have you learned that you might do differently—either about yourself, or about how to run a business in general?

The thought of that is horrible. One of my concerns now is this idea of a consortium, because it almost feels like another business, and I honestly have enough on my plate right now.

You just have to follow your passions and love what you do. That is what is so engaging about entrepreneurship. When you start something you love it—it is the drive, core or seed that determines how you create your business, and your life. There is an emotional and personal connection to your work as an entrepreneur that most people don't find in a job. Some people do, but most people don't.

By Erin Albert

With a job, for most people, they end up compromising fun in order to get paid for work. If we insist that we love what we do instead, rather than hate what we do if we get paid, the world would be a much better place. Most businesses never get the gifts that you can bring to work and to the world. When you start your own business, you have a real chance to create an environment where you absolutely love your work, and in turn, everyone around you can love it too. If you have a great idea and implement it in a way that makes people hate it, what's the point?

That's where values become so important. Values frame the content for creating a business that is full of life. You have a verbal reminder of how to be and how to make whatever it is that you're doing a delightful experience. Chip Conley has a company called Joie de Vivre—the joy of life—and that's also how he treats his employees and customers. You can do this as an employee or entrepreneur too, but as an entrepreneur you have more power to make that happen. As an employee, you'll have more limits. If you love your work, though, that helps. If you're just there for a paycheck, that's really hard to do. We seek joy in our families or volunteerism or other ways when we don't love our work. But it puts a huge stress on us that truly doesn't need to be there. We are here to love and have fun! Some just aren't focused on that, but we all should be.

Did you start your business with your own capital?

Yes, it has been mostly all my own capital. Now I'm in the fortunate place of having a financial angel giving me some help. But, I'm also now in the place where I'm trying to raise capital. Women go to banks to get money, and that is not where you get capital for a business. It's a whole different game to raise capital, as I said before. I think this is a difference between men and women. With men, if they like another guy, they are willing to give him money to run his business. I don't know if it has something to do with the mother in us as women, but there's something where men don't think we can handle the ugliness that can happen in business.

There is a code that must be cracked to get capital. I learned about this at CEO Space, but you have to find someone who is willing to share the secrets with you. Guys have a network, so if you have a relationship with someone, they'll tell you. My dad taught my brother about money, but not me. He assumed I'd grow up, get married, and the man would worry about that. That's changing to some extent, but it is really hard to figure out how to get money unless you have friends with money. Also, the investors out there who have money to give to you are mainly men … about 95% of them are men. Men respond better to other men. It is a relationship that they understand.

It is also my own personal belief that if a man doesn't grow up with a sister, he doesn't really know what to do with women in business or how to treat them. They don't view women as peers. I think a lot of sexual harassment is really men trying to figure out how to relate to women in business, because men treat men differently. It goes back to my previous comment about the ranking thing—men are constantly ranking themselves against each other. When men run into women in business, they either think they are moms or something else but NOT peers. I've seen that in corporations too. Women were well respected by their male peers, so they were treated as part of the guys' club. But, the women didn't perceive the men respected them AT ALL. It's sad in some ways, because women who have done amazing things simultaneously felt absolutely disrespected, but they actually weren't. Men felt they weren't appreciated either.

What about the challenges of the roller coaster income as an entrepreneur?

I think what I found teaching high school kids is that some found entrepreneurship can be a challenge when they realize they need the stability of income and healthcare insurance. When you're an entrepreneur, income goes up and comes down, and it can be a struggle. That's why it is important to save before starting a business. It is going to take some time for the income to come in when starting, unless you're extremely lucky. Understanding income flow is big deal. That, and dealing with ambiguity.

By Erin Albert

Why do you think more single/divorced and widowed women start more businesses than men in their respective categories, and does your theory match your own rationale for starting a business?

I am a serial entrepreneur; that is how I live. I like the freedom and ability to do what I want to do. My first business was actually selling gold jewelry. That was a big deal in the 1960s, because it was the first time you could sell gold outside of a jewelry store. I had a stock of gold jewelry and I'd visit friends and they would buy from me. But it allowed me an income, to enjoy what I was doing, and it was something that was all mine. I was able to be who I actually was at "work."

Also, I think for women with children, it is really tough to leave them behind and go back to the workforce. For example, now I'm watching friends who just had kids re-enter the workforce, and someone else is raising their children. It's not the mother, because she's at work. That is a really painful thing to do. Entrepreneurship gives you both worlds—the ability to make a reasonable living working for yourself and a LOT of control over the kind of life you have in a way you could never do within corporate America as an employee.

What is your personal definition of success, and have you achieved it?

My personal expression of success is fully expressing myself and really feeling like I've made a difference in the lives of others by doing so. I've had moments of this with my teaching and consulting (which in a way is just another form of teaching). When I work with clients, it is always very gratifying to see where they go and how much they can achieve. We just did a strategic planning event for a client; it far exceeded everyone's expectations and went in directions that could not have been predicted. That to me is success.

What else is important to being a single woman entrepreneur that I didn't ask you?

Values are very important to a company. Our company's values are: integrity of the whole, all actions create the conditions that support life, co-creation, curiosity and experimentation. Also lately, with our website design in particular, I've been giving a lot of thought to what it really means to be ethical. I've never had a good description. I've always believed that there are fundamental things that are right that one should do. We tend to go to religion for those things, but that's not perfect either. We are told not to lie, but the minute we do that, we can easily think of situations where we should lie. When you get your values straight and how they fit into the bigger picture by committing to create situations that support life, the appropriate use of other values falls into place for me. This is what I've come to believe.

Kara Allan

Kara Allan & Associates, LLC

Kara *Allan's* clients are CEOs, corporate professionals, lawyers, actors, entrepreneurs, former military personnel and others who are "fashion-challenged." Kara Allan & Associates provides services such as personal shopping, closet organization, wardrobe styling, color consultation and body shape analysis, custom clothing for men and women, group shopping trips, couples styling, interview dressing and corporate image consulting. Her team consists of makeup artists, clothing, shoe and jewelry designers, hair stylists, manicurists, custom shapewear services and bridal beauty services.

Kara Allan & Associates, LLC is a full service Style Concierge that caters to upscale individuals, groups, and corporations. The mission of the company is to inspire and educate clients about how great they can look and feel in their clothes. It is Kara's aspiration to live out her purpose in Christ and express Him by using her abilities and talents to assist others to be their best and have positive interactions with those she comes into contact. Clients are assured VIP treatment with an unmatched level of customer service. Looking *current, stylish and polished is essential for everyone today! Find her on the web at: www.KaraAllan.com.*

Can you describe your business in one sentence?

We change people's lives by changing their wardrobes.

You started two businesses—the first business you started while you were married, and the second business, not married. What were the differences, if any?

Yes. I started my first business in 2001, and I was married. I originally started with web design and presentations, because I did that type of work in my former day job. I closed down that business and then began Kara Allan & Associates, LLC. My husband at the time of my first business wasn't involved in my business at all, so there wasn't any difference starting either business.

What advantages do you think you have as a single business owner that perhaps married business owners do not have?

There are advantages and disadvantages. You have a lot of autonomy. You have the chance to make your own decisions, but you don't necessarily have support, either. If you had a spouse or significant other who also was entrepreneurial or had a complementary skill set, that would be an advantage. Also, as a single, you have to do everything. That's the big thing—you are chief cook and bottle washer! You also have to take care of the kids, the family, and the business—it is all on you.

Do you think business ownership has led you to remain single?

I don't really think of them as related, so, no.

What advice would you give another single woman who is thinking about starting a business?

You have to definitely have the mindset of an entrepreneur. My mom always says that she wants to start a business, and each time I tell her I am going to do this or that, the first question she asks me is if I'm getting paid for it. When you start, you might have to get out and give your skills away for a while. Savings or another income would be helpful, but that's not always a luxury for a single woman.

Also, I would recommend that she talk to someone in the industry who is willing to give her some insight, that way she'll know what she's really getting herself into. At one point, I thought I wanted to be lawyer, so I went to work for a law firm. After that, I was like—HELL NO, I don't want to be a lawyer! I'm glad I had that experience. Just work or intern in the field you're thinking about, because it might not be what you think it is.

What about being a WOMAN business owner?

I see the negative stigmas going away for women in business because women are now starting the most businesses. We are also graduating from college and attending graduate school more than men now too. So, a lot of the 'traditional' stigmas are going away because women now own some of the most successful businesses.

What was the best training you received to prepare you as a business owner?

Being an entrepreneur is in my blood. My father owned property, but he didn't necessarily love it. When I was young, I ran a lemonade stand with some of the other neighborhood kids, and started Kids Incorporated—we'd wash windows and clean houses for money. When I was 12, I got interested in doing makeup. When I was 15, I started working at the mall at several different retailers. I LOVED putting together outfits to help people feel more confident. The hours and the pay weren't great, and the management irked me, but I loved helping customers.

I was in the private sector for a long time working in a day job, and then my mom saw an article on a consultant named Darlene Mathis in the paper who was talking about how wearing certain clothes compliment the wearer and how you should have them in your wardrobe as well. I was talking to my hairdresser about the article (we tell our hairdressers everything anyway, right?) and my hairdresser actually knew this woman, so I got connected! Darlene decided to do a seminar since a lot of people called after seeing her in the article. It was a full day—half of the day we learned how to find someone's best colors, and the other half was spent on applying makeup.

I took this class around 2001, and noticed that other training on how to do image consulting was outrageously expensive and I couldn't afford to travel to the consultants and pay for the classes. So I read every book I could get my hands on around fashion, body typing, and image. I kept working and did other things for 2 years until I came across AICI in 2006, or the Association of Image Consultants International, which has three levels of certification; the First Level Certification (FLC), The Certified Image Professional (CIP) and the Certified Image Master (CIM), of which there are only 8 in the world. It was at a conference where I met Carla Mathis, a CIM. Her company is Body Beautiful. I took two of Carla's Certification classes and loved it! She is truly a professional and a wonderful person. Although I don't have my AICI certification anymore because the cost of maintaining the certification didn't translate to business for me, I still attend some of their trade association meetings. I've had the chance to be part of Stacy London's new venture, Style for Hire (www.styleforhire.com) and I am certified through her company as well. I keep up with my education on fashion, style and business by reading the latest books. I am also a makeup artist; I freelanced for MAC Cosmetics for a few years and Christian Dior Cosmetics as well. The only part of image I don't do is hair, and my daughter is studying cosmetology right now, so I won't have to!

Did you, or are you running your business as a part-time or full-time venture? Why?

I run this business full-time. I'm also a full-time student at George Mason now studying communication.

By Erin Albert

Did you ever take on a partner in either of your businesses?

I never took a partner in this image consulting business, but I did have a partner in my former business. The cool thing about having a partner then was that I started the business, but she ran it. She took care of the books and paperwork. Problem was, when she stopped taking care of everything, I had to. She had other businesses she was developing too, so we decided to shut the business down. I realized I needed to get educated on how to run a business, so I went to the Community Business Partnership in Springfield, VA (www.cbponline.org) and took some great classes by experts on how to start, fund and run a business.

You are willing to learn how to develop a business. What other things are you trying in your business now to expand it?

I'm actually going into business with a friend of mine who has a dance studio in Washington D.C. We're expanding her business into Virginia. She has bachelorette parties and she teaches pole dancing, yoga and is a personal trainer. I'll be offering fashion and image consultations through her business expansion as well. We want to find someone who can run the dance studio too.

How important were mentors in your entrepreneurial career?

Well, I can't say I had any that were directly for entrepreneurship. I had a boss, Barbara Williams, who had a huge positive influence on me. She was classy, she knew her stuff, and she was not a micromanager. She taught me about the importance of how you present yourself in a business setting. There were a LOT of examples of how NOT to present yourself in business that we worked around.

I also have a client now whose husband took over a business and sold it off recently, so I had the chance to talk to him about his business. I've also been connected through them to their interior designer in Miami, so I guess, now that I think about it, I've had more mentors in the past 3-6 months on how to operate a business than I've ever had.

Did you start your business with your own capital?

Yes. It wasn't that expensive to start. I started it for around $500—I had to have a business license, incorporate, and other things. My friend built my website for me.

How important are your social and personal networks to the success of your business?

Networking is HUGE. One of the things I did last year was join Success in the City (www.successinthecity.com), a local group in Washington, D.C. The lady who founded it is Cynthia de Lorenzi—she's so fabulous and calls herself the head diva. The networking group is founded on women doing better in nurturing and supporting each other—we socialize differently than men, who play golf, as an example. Talking and nurturing relationships are how business gets done with women ... that's what we do. A lot of referrals and work I do now is because of having these different relationships with other networking groups. The other networking group I participate in is Work it Girl! Networking, headed by Supergirl Teresa Young, (www.workitgirlnetworking.com). They have great speakers come and talk about their business or whatever their passions are during lunch. There's no membership fee, you just pay for lunch and meet some great women!

What is your personal definition of success, and have you achieved it?

I don't know that I have a definition yet. For me, success is not all about the money. It instead is about who you help and the relationships you make along the way. For me, the best part about what I do is that I have the power to change someone's life by improving the way they feel about how they look. That effects their *life*. People want to pooh-pooh style and fashion, but image really does make a difference. People who look like bums don't become the CEO of Microsoft. You don't have to be a GQ model, but you can change the way you look and improve your life. If I'm able to do that and support my family, that to me is success.

By Erin Albert

What didn't I ask you about you and your business that you wanted me to?

I have been listening to Robert Kiyosaki on a CD called *Choose to Be Rich*. I actually had it for a while, but forgot about it and then I went back to listen to it again. He talks about people who are poor, rich and middle class and how they think differently, not good or bad, just how they think. For me, I've been thinking a lot about having the entrepreneurial mindset. People who have made it big found an unmet need and filled it. He challenges us to think about what we really do and how we really think and who we can help. He also suggested one of the ways to get rich is to have three different piggy banks—say if you have a $100 in income, you should put $10 in savings, $10 in tithing and $10 in investments. If you lose your investments, you have your savings to fall back on. The tithing can be giving to your church or your charity, but you are giving and that will be reciprocated.

I think this is similar to being an entrepreneur. What are you giving to other people? How are you planning for that in your future as well? Everyone can lose everything in one day no matter who they are. An entrepreneur has to plan and save, but not be afraid of failure. Nine out of 10 businesses fail; true, but one business succeeds. You have to have that resilience to carry yourself through the planning and potential of failure, and realize that if an idea or a business didn't come out right the first time, it might have nothing to do with you or your work. It might be bad luck, poor timing, or something else you had no control over. The one thing you can control is your resilience. Having the resiliency to get back up is key. Too many nos will eventually get you that much closer to a yes!

Niquelle R. Allen, Esq.

Butterfly Consignment

Niquelle R. Allen *is an attorney, mediator, and entrepreneur. Ms. Allen owns Butterfly Consignment, an upscale ladies' boutique in Indianapolis, Indiana, where fashion has evolved. She is also Of Counsel at Fleming Stage, LLC law firm and owns Mediation Works, LLC, a professional mediation, title closing, and notary service. Prior to beginning her entrepreneurial journey, Ms. Allen was an in-house legal counsel at Eli Lilly and Company. A Gary, Indiana native, Ms. Allen has also worked as an attorney at Ice Miller, LLP and served as a judicial law clerk. In 2006, Ms. Allen was awarded the Up & Coming Lawyer—Leadership in Law Award by* The Indiana Lawyer. *Ms. Allen attended Vanderbilt University Law School and is a proud alumnus of Tennessee State University, where she graduated magna cum laude with a B.S. in political science. She is active in the community and is a member of the National Coalition of 100 Black Women, Alpha Kappa Alpha Sorority, Inc., and the Marion County Bar Association.*

Single. Women. Entrepreneurs.

Butterfly Consignment, an upscale ladies' boutique, is a place where women can save money, make money, recycle, and give back to the community. Butterfly Consignment offers pre-loved (gently-used), "N" love (unsold new inventory from boutiques), and made with love (handmade jewelry, handbags, body care, etc.) merchandise. Butterfly Consignment has a spectacular selection of better to designer apparel, handbags, shoes, jewelry, perfume, and accessories in a variety of styles (casual to formal) and sizes (petite to plus). Select vintage pieces (jewelry/handbags) are also available. It is located at 6697 E. 82nd Street, Indianapolis, IN and is located online at: www.shopBfly.com. The company also has a Facebook page (butterflyconsignment), a Twitter feed (@shopbfly) and has pictures at flickr (www.flickr.com/shopbfly.com).

What advantages do you think you have as a single solo business owner that married people don't have?

As a single woman, I was able to focus all of my time, resources, and attention to the creation and continued success of the business. I had to crawl as a caterpillar before I could grow wings and begin to fly as a butterfly. In the beginning, I had to do it all by myself: marketing, media relations, event planning, networking, sales, accounting, cleaning, etc. Some women with families may not be able to fully dedicate themselves to a start-up business due to their family responsibilities. Others may not be willing to take the same risk to start a business in this type of economy, due to the financial needs of their families.

So, is the name of your business also a symbol of your own entrepreneurial metamorphosis? How did you come up with this (awesome) symbol?

I have always loved butterflies because they represent evolution and beauty. I am a butterfly in my own right. I have evolved academically, professionally and creatively, and my wings are in full span. As an attorney, mediator, entrepreneur and self-described 'closet consultant', my passions flutter together in harmony. I named the store Butterfly, because I wanted to change the way fashionistas look at consignment—by creating a beautiful boutique where they can save money, make money, recycle and give back to the community. Fashion has evolved, and it's about more than just looking good.

What about disadvantages to a single woman owning a business?

Being single also meant that I was completely on my own. I did not have a second income to fall back on.

Do you think business ownership has led you to remain single?

I don't think that business ownership has had any effect on my marital status. I was an extremely busy and active person before owning my business and predict that won't change regardless of my marital status.

What advice would you give another single woman who is thinking about starting a business?

Pray. Dream big. Pray. Plan purposefully. Pray. Take action. Pray.

What was the best training you received to prepare you as a business owner?

My upbringing, educational and practical work experience prepared me to be successful in any endeavor. Also, talking to other business owners, friends, and family encouraged me to utilize my education and experience. Once my mind was made up, other places like the Business Ownership Initiative of Indiana (BOI)* were also key in providing guidance, information and additional resources.

*[The Business Ownership Initiative, or BOI, is part of the Central Indiana Women's Business Center, and part of the Small Business Administration at the state level. BOI offers classes on thinking about becoming an entrepreneur, to building a business plan, to networking and other skills for budding and new entrepreneurs. For more information on who they are and the great things they do, logon to www.businessownership.org.]

Single. Women. Entrepreneurs.

Did you, or are you running your business as a part-time or full-time venture? Why?

I am running my business full-time, while also working as an attorney.

Why are you doing both? (What is your philosophy behind doing both?)

I have wanted to be an attorney since I was 8 years old. I love solving problems and working with people. I don't think that I have to choose between using the left side of my brain or the right side. I like to have my analytical and creative juices flowing at the same time.

If you had to start another business, what have you learned that you might do differently—either about yourself, or about how to run a business in general?

The most important thing that I have learned is that no matter how well thought out your plan is, things will come up that cause you to modify or change your plan along the way. You have to be flexible and practical to make it work.

How important were mentors in your entrepreneurial career?

I had several mentors who guided me along the way. The Business Ownership Initiative of Indiana was also important in the process. None of my mentors per se encouraged me to start a business; however, it was something I always had in the back of my mind since the day I walked into my first consignment store in college. I love consignment shopping and wanted to do it because it's fun for me.

Did you start your business with your own capital?

I used my own capital, as well as a line of credit from Old National Bank.

Was the line of credit difficult to obtain, especially in this economic recession?

No—because I had excellent personal credit.

How important are your social and personal networks to the success of your business?

As an attorney and social butterfly, I have done tons of networking over the years. The relationships I built have helped build my business tremendously. I am involved in several organizations and my colleagues have supported me in the business. For example, my Alpha Kappa Alpha sorority chapter hosted an event at my store last week and it was a great turnout; 50 plus women came and it was my best sales day to date!

Why do you think more single/divorced and widowed women start more businesses than men in their respective categories, and does your theory match your own rationale for starting a business?

We are taught to put others' needs before our own. When a woman is single, divorced, or widowed, she has a unique opportunity to stop and do something for herself.

What is your personal definition of success, and have you achieved it?

Success is dreaming and taking action to make your dreams come true. I am successful.

Julia Aquino

The How Factor, Inc.

Julia Aquino *is a single mom of a 7-year-old son and has two dogs that were rescued from shelters. She was a financial analyst, manager and COO in the corporate world and currently owns The How Factor, Inc. Her expertise comes from helping troubled and startup companies become more efficient, both financially and productively. Bottom Line: She has a wonderful little family, an amazing group of friends around her, and loves what she does every day—and for that, she is eternally grateful.*

The How Factor, Inc. was established to assist businesses with growth and sustainability through the documentation of efficient processes and procedures in Operations Manuals—oftentimes referred to as Policy and Procedure Manuals. The How Factor also educates and offers webinars for smaller companies that wish to document their company on their own. The company website can be found at: www.howfactor.com.

Single. Women. Entrepreneurs.

Can you describe your business in one sentence?

We help companies add structure in the midst of chaos.

You've got a phenomenal tag line in your email footer: "If it's only in your head ... it's only a hobby!" Can you share where that tag line came from?

It actually came out of a conversation I had with my business coach. We were talking about how entrepreneurs know everything about their business, but if something happened to them, they'd no longer have a business, because the business could not function without them. Therefore, the business really wasn't a business; it was a hobby. It's all in their heads and not documented anywhere. If you are in a hobby—if you build model trains or arrange flowers, for example, you never really document how you do it—you just do it. In business, however, if you truly want a sustainable, practical business moving forward, you must document what you're doing in order to go forward. Otherwise, it is still only a hobby. When I say this, the light bulb goes off in many entrepreneurs' heads. If you ask small business owners, 99% of them have nothing documented. Shockingly, 95% of them don't have business plans either. That just frightens me. I don't know how someone can start a business without a plan.

What advantages do you think you have as a divorced solo business owner that your married counterparts don't have?

From my experience, I learned the following: I got married, and worked in corporate America about 50-60 hours per week and became an executive. Then, I moved out of corporate America to have and care for a baby. When I wanted to go back to work, the conversation then was—what about managing my child, a spouse and work? The expectation from my spouse was not aligned with my desire to pursue my dreams. My spouse at the time didn't mean to ask about this balance selfishly, but on the other hand, if you don't have a supportive spouse, there are limitations on what you can do.

By Erin Albert

Now that I'm not married, I can work until 11 o'clock at night, and I can work without guilt. I can take care of business without worrying about a spouse's expectations, which allows me the space to build my dream. Now, just worrying about me, my child, and my dogs is easier than worrying about another person who has different expectations of how things should be because their dreams and expectations are different than mine.

What about disadvantages?

As a single mom, when my son needs to be picked up from school because he's sick, I have to do it. The business gets pushed to the side, especially for a child. It can be difficult to explain to clients that you have to cancel at the last minute. Luckily, I have great clients and they understand. Most understand that as a single mom, my 7-year-old child is a priority.

I've also learned that a single mom still is responsible for the majority of what takes place with children. Even though my son has a great dad who is responsible, I still must make sure my child has his doctor and dentist appointments completed, is picked up from school on time, etc. I take that role as mom.

Do you think business ownership has led you to remain single?

I'm not married, but I have a significant other. The difference in this relationship is that he is hugely supportive and accepting. On a day I'm completely swamped with work, he'll come over and walk the dogs. When my grocery list is full, he'll come over, get the groceries and put them away for me. I also talked to him about going back for my M.B.A., and shared with him my concerns that would occur with me being gone on weekends to attend classes. He already volunteered to come over and take care of the dogs. He's incredibly proud of what I do, and has already helped me put into place the things that would need to happen in order for me to pursue my dream this fall to further my education.

What advice would you give another single woman who is thinking about starting a business?

Go for it! I think when it is your calling or passion, you need to move mountains and part oceans to get there. Of course, don't do it without a business plan, and here's why. Four out of five businesses fail within 5 years of starting, but, I think we could get this down to two out of five if everyone wrote a business plan, followed it, and updated it as necessary. If you actually go through the planning process—do a SWOT analysis and really understand your competition, you can create a business AROUND the potential obstacles and know you have to resolve issues before you just jump in. What happens is that people have a great idea and just start doing it without thinking through the roadblocks. If you have a plan for getting around roadblocks, your chances of success and sustainability are MUCH greater. Without a business plan, some businesses are also grossly underfunded. Then, the passion or great idea becomes a nightmare, because they had not thought through the business concept.

I work 12-hour days and I wonder if I can pay the bills next week. I am constantly looking for different options to grow my business in order to pay the bills. But, even during the worst parts of my business development, I'm still motivated, passionate and willing to go forward. Without that passion, you're in trouble. I don't care how great your business is, no one is successful in 30 days or even a year. Sometimes it takes 5 years to become successful. You have to have the willingness to persevere.

What was the best training you received to prepare you as a business owner?

Corporate America. I think that dealing with all the different personalities and putting out fires in corporate America served me well to learn what I do—by working in organizations that were a complete mess. I was hired to fix the mess and improve the mess. Within the mess, there's always a solution. I'm an analyst. I found a best process to fix something within a company, and then trained people on the new process. However, I slowly watched people start returning to their old ways, until I started documenting processes. That is where my training came from. In corporate America, I worked with companies that had either a large business, or large businesses within a bigger business, and there is no option but to succeed. I worked for some great companies and not so great companies.

What makes a company great?

I think what made the great companies great was clear vision and mission—and respect for their employees. Great companies had good communication with employees and empowered their people to do what needed to be done. A lot of people had great companies at one time, but they just lost their way; they became successful and they had NO IDEA why they were successful, until they changed their formula. And, in that change of formula, they lost what it was that actually made them successful in the first place. Part of that all goes back to clear vision and mission. (And a plan!)

Are you running your business as a part-time or full-time venture?

I am full-time. I'm not sure how people do it part-time, because it seeps into all aspects of your life. I've had a couple ventures, and even this business, which I first started intending them to be part-time. I'll give you an example from my life: I started a part-time gift basket business. What happens when you're only doing it on the side is that you start doing it 4 hours a day. But, something will arise when you need to start putting in 6 hours per day. When work creep happens, something else in your life must give. Usually, it is your children, your spouse, or something that you intended to give your full and undivided attention. Then, you have increasing frustration between doing "what you need to do" and letting someone else down. In that case someone is always neglected. Either way, you can't win. I'd make my gift baskets when people needed them. Then, I had more orders for corporate gift baskets for a company, so I had to hire a nanny. Then the corporate orders for one company turned into 3 companies. Then, 80 boxes were being delivered to my house and I had 4 weeks of full-time work to do, and it was NO LONGER part-time. It was no longer fun, either, and not planned. That is the temptation of a part-time business; when you work part-time and you get these great opportunities, you don't want to turn them down. Then, there arrives a tipping point. You need to either do this full-time, or not. You can't do it part-time anymore.

So, I opened a store and sold gift baskets for 3 years. When the economy started turning bad, we sold the business. My point is this: when you're creating a business full-time, you're creating expectations with your clients and family. When I create something, I'm creating it because I have long-term goals, vision, retirement plans, and an exit strategy. I can't get to that with part-time work. That doesn't mean that eventually I wouldn't like to work part-time and have 50 people under me. But I also realize that won't happen immediately when first building a business.

Besides, in my soul, I'm definitely 100% an entrepreneur. I was speaking to a recruiter friend recently and shared with her that I don't know what I'd do if I actually had to go back to work. She replied that I would be tough to find a job for—because although I'm bright and I'm good at what I do, I need continual challenge. There would be no issue on finding a job; but instead, the issue would be finding a place to *stay*. I need a constant challenge while moving forward and asking myself what's next. Sitting at a desk and watching someone's financials, for example, I'd end up leaving in six months. I'd need to find a dynamic *entrepreneurial* company to work for, if I could find one.

How important were mentors in your entrepreneurial career?

They are more important now versus the past. I don't recall any specific mentors, but I had amazing bosses. In my role now and because of the level of people I deal with, I have a business coach and a spiritual life coach. I also have some strategic alliances around me that are beautifully powerful, open and giving. I am surrounded by mentors and support now. But, I think as an entrepreneur, that's key.

Did you start your business with your own capital?

I used all my own capital. I have one business credit card. There are no loans, now! When I had my gift store, I had loans, and I'm still repaying those loans. I just didn't want to put myself in that position again. Unless I had angel investors who were clear on the vision and goals of my business, I might consider that source for capital, but I wouldn't start a business again on credit. When you go outside of your financial plan and budget, you're in trouble. You don't want to be underfunded, but if you do use funding, you need to stick to your budget. You can't just want something and have it. For example, when you open a retail store, you don't have to buy everything brand new. You can buy used equipment and still get the same effect. If you buy the shiny new equipment, what happens when you don't bring in the money?

The other major financial item with business plans is: be realistic. I've written about 20 business plans in my life (my degrees are in finance and accounting). Every six months, I look at my financial goals and make changes if necessary. If I'm not where I was expected to be, I need to change my numbers going forward to account for where I've been and where I'm going in order to create realistic expectations. I think women are afraid of the numbers because they don't understand them, or they aren't pretty and they don't want to look at them. It's OK if they aren't pretty because they do tell you where to go. If you don't look at them, you can end up in shock (and out of business). However, if you look at them at least twice a year, you can adjust for the rest of the year ahead of time. Be proactive instead of reactive.

What is your personal definition of success, and have you achieved it?

My personal definition is having a balanced life and financially being able to support myself while being able to do what I love. I'm half way there. I'm still working on the work/life balance, and I'm still working on being completely financially independent, but I love what I do and I'm very clear on my vision. The balance is coming. I see glimpses of balance, but it is a choice too. For example, it is a choice to shut your computer off. It is a choice for me to not answer the phone when my son comes home from school. I can also choose for him to sit in the loft while I'm sending emails. When I make the choice, I can go back to work at 8 p.m. at night. When my son is present, I'm present with him from 5:30 p.m. until he goes to bed. He knows that. When he comes home at 3:30 or 4 with the nanny—he does his homework, but at 5:30, he gets my full attention until bedtime.

He's very patient. He'll also call me on it too. He'll say, "Mom, it's my time." Or, if there is something major I have to take care of, I'll tell him in advance. I'm open and communicative with him. There are 1-2 days during the week when he's with his dad and I can work 12-hour days if I want to and I do, so I can be present with him when he is with me.

What didn't I ask you that you think is important to share with others?

I want to emphasize to other women entrepreneurs the following: be sure to document what you do every day. It creates a sustainable organization. When I speak in front of women's groups, I tell them that they never want to have to choose between their mothers and their businesses. If mom needs you to care for her for a month, for example, someone else can duplicate what you do in your business if you've been documenting what it is that you actually do on a daily basis. Then, someone else can run your business and you can care for your mom. A sustainable business can be created when you document what you do.

Andrea Bloom

ConnectWell

Andrea Bloom *is a seasoned executive with over 20 years of business experience including 15 years spent in the health care industry in various product development, marketing, business development and consulting roles. She has worked for leading health care companies, medical device start-ups and health related non-profits (Juvenile Diabetes Research Foundation, American Heart Association, Diabetic Youth Foundation, Playworks and Wellness City Challenge). She continues to be an active research contributor to the Health Horizons practice area at Institute for the Future, a prominent Palo Alto think tank. Andrea's background includes marketing in both the U.S. and international arenas targeting consumers, physicians, hospitals and retailers. She spent 3 years in product development and 5 years in the international division of a major health care company introducing blood glucose monitoring technology to remote parts of the developing world and enabling self-management of diabetes for the first time in many countries. Andrea worked as a diabetes industry consultant as a Principal at Close Concerns and Cogent Reimbursement Strategies before founding her own consultancy, Diabetes Insights. In additional to diabetes, Andrea has a broad knowledge of the health care landscape having worked in a number of disease states for medical device, drug delivery, pharmaceutical and lab equipment companies and on wellness, prevention and disease management programs. She has a deep understanding of health care reimbursement involving payers, providers and government policies. At the beginning of 2010, Andrea founded ConnectWell to leverage her experience-base in health care and create an educational program that teaches sustainable wellness practices for life-long success in eating, activity and a balanced lifestyle. Andrea's education includes a Master of Business Administration from Harvard Business School and a Bachelor of Arts in Economics from University of California, Berkeley with departmental honors, high distinction in general scholarship and Phi Beta Kappa.*

ConnectWell partners with organizations to select and engage employees who demonstrate "readiness" to embrace wellness practices. Their wellness programs support people across the spectrum of health promotion—eating, activity, life skills and balance. ConnectWell's offering focuses on addressing preventable illnesses by empowering individuals through wellness education, and engaging them in activities and exercises to promote and reinforce healthy habit formation. ConnectWell's unique approach enrolls people who are "ready" to embrace wellness practices and engages them in the context of their household values and life goals. The approach is integrative in that the programming threads through all aspects of life to create consistency in behavior patterns that drive positive health outcomes. ConnectWell's household-centered approach reaches beyond standard worksite wellness programs by extending the program to family members representing up to two-thirds of the employer "covered" population. ConnectWell utilizes proven approaches to wellness practices and reaches a widespread population to achieve sustainable reductions in health care costs while enhancing productivity and overall well-being.

By Erin Albert

Could you describe your business in one sentence?

ConnectWell is a wellness education and programming company that reaches people through employers to teach and engage the "ready" population in sustainable wellness practices for life-long success in eating, activity and a balanced life-style.

What advantages do you think you have as a divorced/solo business owner that married business owners don't have?

I think the main advantage is that I am completely independent in my thinking. As a single woman, you don't have to counterbalance your partner's view of what YOU should be doing.

What about disadvantages?

There could be financial disadvantages. It depends upon where you are in your career. There could be more financial disadvantages because you're the only income earner. For me, that's really not the case. I'm further along in my career and have an experience base that is significant. I already launched a business as an independent consultant and my ex-spouse helps support my family. I am fortunate to have an element of that financial freedom. The time is right for me to launch my new business, ConnectWell. I'm in the startup phase of this business and have exclusively focused on it now in 2010. I hope to start gaining visibility for this business 4Q10 and I intend to generate revenue in 2011.

Why this type of business, and why now?

I was thinking about launching the business for a long time. I have been in the diabetes industry since 1993 and watched this epidemic growing while in the industry and it became troubling. From a personal values standpoint, I decided I'd rather prevent diabetes from happening than focus on treatment. I had been operating as an independent consultant, which helped me develop confidence to start a bigger business. I broadened my experience beyond diabetes and I'm still part of a think tank. All of these experiences augmented my view of ConnectWell, which in turn helped me create the vision for this company. I also volunteered at a diabetes camp in 2008. The next year I brought my kids so they could see the impact of this disease on others. You have to stay on top of diabetes and teach kids with type 1 diabetes how to manage it. I kept thinking to myself, if I could help kids at diabetes camp figure out how to manage their disease, I could certainly train adults how to prevent type 2 diabetes from happening in the first place. This idea also provided me with the vision to start my business.

Also, I had a career break. I was on a fast track career path in the corporate world after coming out of Harvard Business School, until my second pregnancy. It turned out that I was pregnant with twins. Having twins was truly a gift, because it forced me to focus not only on my family, but it also changed my view of my work in the corporate world. I then worked as a consultant, which in turn gave me an independent viewpoint, working across companies and over the entire spectrum of diabetes.

Do you think business ownership has led you to remain single?

I am in a stable, long-term relationship with another entrepreneur. He's completely supportive of what I'm doing. I think you have to bring other entrepreneurs into your life. I need to have someone who is supportive and optimistic. I've learned so much, and continue to learn from him on how to think like a CEO.

As an entrepreneur, you have to be around nurturing people. All the odds are against you, so you really need fans and supporters and like-minded thinkers that tell you that, "You can do this!" which in turn gives you the energy to keep on plugging away at your idea and vision.

What advice would you give another single woman who is thinking about starting a business?

She has to have a lot of confidence in her capabilities and the concept she's developing. Most people are going to try and knock you down. You've got to be really strong and know your own capabilities in order to move your idea forward. You have to be ready for rejection; you'll hear "no" over and over again. You're also not going to have a big company behind you with nearly infinite resources. You have to evolve the business idea and move it forward as you get market information in order for it to become successful. It is important to always keep learning as well.

What about your education? Did that play a role in you becoming an entrepreneur?

Over half of the graduates of Harvard Business School start their own companies. That gave me a lot of confidence—that I was trained to do this—and at this point in my life, I knew I wanted to start a business. I also took an entrepreneurial management class at Harvard, and learned that I have the bootstrapping, startup mentality. Harvard also has a really strong outreach program to their alumni. They also offer a Virtual Learning Series to the alums, and broadcast the webinar series, which I attend. Recently, they had Lynda Applegate (a professor of entrepreneurial management at Harvard Business School) discuss entrepreneurship. That course gave me that extra momentum and encouragement to move forward and support my business idea. Although I earned my M.B.A. when I was in my twenties (pre-marriage, pre-family), Harvard Business School continues to offer me great resources to start and move ahead with my business.

What about being a single WOMAN business owner? Do you think it is easier, the same, or harder than being a single man starting a business?

I think it is actually easier to be a woman business owner today than work in corporate America as woman. The pay/equity issue still exists. Also, the corporate environment is so inflexible on how the work is bundled, even today. It is very restrictive. In corporate America, in order to be on the fast track, a lot of face and travel time are required. Furthermore, people in corporate America make judgments on your gender, your marital status, whether or not you have kids relative to what they think you can do. It is very hard for a corporation to tap into your entire personal talent base because they decide what you can or cannot do, and it is very rigid.

I work just as hard if not harder than I did in corporate America now as a business owner, but I work on my schedule. I work when my kids are asleep, and now I have to be even more productive during my work time. I can schedule work around my family life and not have it negatively impact my work or my family life. I schedule my meetings with people I need to meet with and it is very fluid. I can work on a weekend when the kids are with their father, and it works much better with my life—and no one is judging me based on my parental responsibilities or how I spend my time.

I think this is a big piece of why entrepreneurship works well for women. Women plateau in corporate America at levels not fulfilling for them, because the corporation doesn't maximize the skills of women with families by providing flexible work arrangements. Also, there are so many politics inside corporate America that you spend more time thinking about having to work through and around the internal system that work isn't as efficient. As an entrepreneur, I just get things done! I get so much more work done by working at a faster and more productive pace this way—I don't have to work through the politics.

What was the best training you received to prepare you as a business owner, other than your M.B.A.?

I have role models in my family who are entrepreneurs. We've done this in our family for generations. I'm trained to be in corporate America, but I can transfer these skills to creating and growing my own business. My dad is a physician and started in group practice, then went into private practice. He broke out and started his own practice and then expanded it into a group practice partnership. They had a common vision of how to move it forward together. That was important to me. I could see how having his own practice gave him flexibility in his schedule to take more trips and spend time with his family. He wasn't restricted by corporate philosophy.

I think this had an important influence on me, because I learned by watching him that entrepreneurs have more freedom to design their lives. As an entrepreneur, I feel like I have more control to design a total life; people are multi-dimensional. Corporate America is about getting a few weeks of vacation and that's it, but entrepreneurship allows me to have this freedom to design my life and work in concert with all dimensions of my life.

Also, relative to my education gearing me for entrepreneurship, I went to UC Berkeley as an undergrad and currently live in the Bay Area. I tap into their alumni events as well. They offer a Women in Leadership conference with entrepreneurship and healthcare panels. Attending the panel discussions has been very helpful, as entrepreneurs are very willing to share their challenges and struggles. I love these panels, because they are encouraging and provide ideas to help you move forward rather than just telling you something won't work.

How about being both a mom and an entrepreneur?

It is so much easier to be an entrepreneur and mom than being a mom in corporate America. People expect me to be a mom as an entrepreneur because my business is wellness. I talk a lot about kids and positive role modeling by adults around eating as part of creating an environment for successful wellness practices. I share the motherhood piece much more freely and comfortably as a business owner rather than I did in corporate America, because talking about being a mom in corporate America sounds like I'm not committed to the company. It has become an asset to be a mother as an entrepreneur, whereas in corporate America it was a liability.

Did you take on a partner in your business at any time?

My new business did not originally start with just me. I originally started this business with a neighbor, who was already an entrepreneur. We made some progress together, but she had other businesses going on at the time, and she decided to focus on them. I told her I was entirely committed to this concept, so I'd like to transfer the business to me, and bought her out of the business. Now, it is just me.

If you had to start another business, what have you learned that you might do differently—either about yourself, or about how to run a business in general?

I think the ownership piece I would do differently if I had to start over or start again. Knowing what I know now, it is hard to have a partnership. You need someone to set a strategic direction and having a partner sometimes slows you down. But, through this first business I started, having a partner initially was a blessing, because I don't think I would have had the confidence to do this alone. I gained the confidence when I started to get more into the concept and by the time I bought my partner out of the business, I was able to reshape the vision of the business to a place that is a better fit with the market need. Starting with someone else gave me the confidence to drive the business on my own. Owning a business truly is experiential learning. You have to go through the experience in the real world to truly learn how to run a business. It is a process of doing, constantly learning, and understanding how you are going to assimilate new information into the business.

How important were mentors in your entrepreneurial career?

I wouldn't say I have one mentor. I have different role models in my life. My father has been a good role model, as a business oriented physician—practicing good medicine and running a solid business. I find role models in a lot of places. For example, Harvard has outreach programs to women alumni who are in career transition. When I went to my 15-year business school reunion, I enrolled in the Charting Your Course program where I spent 2 days with 48 women, and they had good role models there; some were entrepreneurs. I have kept in touch with some women on those panels and ask them questions on occasion even now. That has been very helpful. Another good role model is my partner in life. As I previously mentioned, he's an entrepreneur too. Even though

By Erin Albert

I'm self-funding my own business and he has venture capital for his, there are a lot of other issues around entrepreneurship that are similar between his business and mine. I've learned a lot just by watching him go through his experiences.

How important are your social and personal networks to the success of your business?

I do think networks are important, and right now I'm learning what networks I should tap into.

Why do you think more single/divorced and widowed women start more businesses than men in their respective categories, and does your theory match your own rationale for starting a business?

I think flexibility is a big piece. I also think women may have a broader vision than men because they have more career breaks. They exit their corporate roles (especially when becoming a mother) and it gives them the chance to create a new vision for their careers. I think sometimes you have to take yourself out of the corporate world to see the new vision. You can think independently outside of corporate America. In the corporate world, you are trained to think within the corporation. You're not supposed to use your full capabilities. But when you remove yourself from that mentality, you can start seeing more opportunities and how to solve problems in an entrepreneurial way. Women have that advantage because of the career breaks.

What is your personal definition of success, and have you achieved it?

You have to define success in your own terms. My definition of success is to do interesting, high impact work, while also enjoying the other dimensions of my life. One piece of that life is being engaged in my children's lives. Also, success to me is giving myself time for my relationship, my friends and being involved in my community, and taking care of my personal health. I have achieved that. I am doing very interesting high impact work and am fully engaged in all aspects of my life, so I have achieved my own personal definition of success.

What else hasn't been asked that you feel passionately about sharing?

I feel really strongly about this: I want women to know that their gender does NOT have to hold them back. Whatever a woman wants to do, independent of her personal relationship status, or deciding to have kids, her choices should not hold her back. She must believe in herself and find the right environment to utilize her skills, and if that means she should be an entrepreneur, great. If she can find what she wants to be in corporate America, great. But as an entrepreneur, you create the corporate culture and decide when you work, who you hire, what types of people you will partner with, etc. and it is liberating to be able to create your environment, rather than trying to fit into a corporate structure and culture that already exits.

Tracey Brame

West Point Financing

Tracey Brame *is an Indianapolis native from birth. At age 9, she declared she was going to a top 10 school, putting the* Newsweek *list under her bed. At age 18, she was accepted to every top ten school in the country. She settled into West Point because it felt closest to her Pentecostal upbringing. After leaving the Army, she created an IT recruiting firm, working almost exclusively for EMC2's channel division. The downturn in IT during the early 2000s left Tracey looking for a new angle. In 2007, she started* **West Point Financing***, a national equipment lease and financing firm. Her biggest deal to date is designing a $50 million vehicle lease program for the city of Indianapolis' Department of Public Works, Indianapolis Metropolitan Police Department and Indianapolis Fire Department. She is in current contention for leasing agent for one of the state's largest hospital systems. Her company is online at: www.westpointfinancing.com.*

Single. Women. Entrepreneurs.

What advantages do you think you have as a solo business owner that married people don't have?

I *have* to succeed. No one is standing behind me with a safety net in case things don't work out.

What about disadvantages?

I don't have a safety net. It's a dual-edged sword. When I network, no one else in the room has vested interest in talking about my company except me.

Do you think business ownership has led you to remain single?

No. Once I get more experience under my belt, I will settle down.

What advice would you give another single woman who is thinking about starting a business?

Make sure you have the guts to do this. If you doubt that you have the resolve, you may lack it. There is no crying in baseball or ownership. Own your success, and own your failure.

Do you think there are advantages/disadvantages to being a single business owner? Do you think it is harder, or easier?

I do not think that it is either. You access your strengths. If you do not have a safety net, then make sure you have more liquidity than the next person.

How did you discover and access your own strengths?

I've always assessed what it takes for me to survive—a failed marriage, West Point, etc., throughout those situations I never lowered by lifestyle. Characteristics about me that prevent my failing are my strengths. One of them would be a belief that I can do what anyone else can do. If John can jump out of a plane and not die, I can do it too. If they survived and had the brains to walk away, I can too. I can do anything an above average person can do. I admit I can't do what Michael Jordan can do, but I could if I worked hard at it.

By Erin Albert

I had a superior upbringing with my grandparents. It is amazing that people can get through this life and I marvel at how they do without having known my grandparents. I had a fantastic upbringing. It was a good foundation, so when I arrived at West Point I could handle it because my grandfather was a preacher and had a lot of rules too. I broke some rules but I didn't go bad—I basically assumed that rules were reasonable and unless it was being imposed on me because I'm black or female, I should follow them. Little things like that gave me strength so that even when I'm in a situation where there are no rules, I create rules to give myself order.

What about being a single WOMAN business owner?
Do you think it is easier, the same, or harder than being a
single man starting a business?
I think those who have someone helping with the ancillary roles in life are at an advantage, male or female. The challenge with being black or female is that some Caucasians and men will test you in unnerving ways to tip you off your course. Of course, they do this to each other too. It is just part of the game. During half time and breaks, having a cheerleader squarely in your court has to be worth something.

What was the best training you received to prepare you as a
business owner?
West Point taught me what the 'man's game board' looks like. I am in a male dominated field where frankly African Americans tend not to tread. I think that my education and upbringing taught me to perform well when alone among strangers in the room.

What else, if anything, did your military training play a role
in your entrepreneurial career path?
You can't quit West Point. You can, but your family is disappointed. You'll always be the daughter who quit West Point. You can't quit. Some people get kicked out, but most people don't quit. The idea that you have to hang in there helped me as an entrepreneur. There

were years where I had negative tax returns—negative $25K. I was bleeding and couldn't get a break—but I couldn't quit. Some other person is doing it, so I can. Not sure that's healthy, but I just can't quit.

Did you, or are you running your business as a part-time or full-time venture? Why?

Full-time. I cannot waste time doing most things part-time.

Did you take on a partner in your business at any time?

I have not taken on a partner. I am signing up referral partners.

How important are mentors in your entrepreneurial career?

They are immensely important. Successful men are helping me more than any other group. This is not an attraction issue but a mentor issue. I appreciate getting good answers to my questions.

Did you start your business with your own capital? Did you try to obtain capital from other sources?

My capital. No.

Why not?

I couldn't obtain capital. If you start a service company based upon yourself, it is not financeable. I'm a saver and try not to spend the money I have. I'm irritated if I have to touch my savings. As a single parent, I have to keep a lot of money on hand, and when I don't have that there, I'm stressed. I ran near empty and then took off just in time. All the time I'm thinking I can do it—I just haven't had my break yet—I can do it.

How important are your social and personal networks to the success of your business?

Social and personal networks are not a factor. Professional networks are key.

So, you view your networks differently? If so, why?

Easy. You can go to NAWBO (the National Association of Women Business Owners) and hug everyone, but I feel it is a professional association. If you need help, they'll help you. I had a question and asked another NAWBO member and talked with her for 7 minutes one day before work. She put me on the right path; that was good. I professionally network with them but don't hang out with them at night because I need to be with my son, who is a teenager. There's no expectation of me to drop by friends' houses during their family hours. I wouldn't readily talk to my professional network about my personal problems—that's the difference between a social network and a business network to me.

Why do you think more single/divorced and widowed women start more businesses than men in their respective categories, and does your theory match your own rationale for starting a business?

We are told that we can't do things more often. Once you have tried the whole love thing and realized that your goals will be unfulfilled if not filled by you, you activate. I do not need a man to be happy. My company is like a child. The business world is the surrogate father. I can do this alone. When people say you need a husband, they're saying you can't make it on your own. Women don't need to have a husband and don't need to cook. We are told what we have to do, and I reject that. I always have. My grandmother told me to go to a specific large company and get a job and not go to West Point, but I went anyway, and now that large company is laying off thousands of employees. Women must focus on what they want and can do, not what society explicitly and implicitly suggests that they need to do.

What is your personal definition of success, and have you achieved it?

I want to be debt free and independently wealthy. It won't ensure happiness, but it will curb certain fears. I am on my way.

Katasha Butler

K Sherrie + Company Planning Atelier

Katasha Butler *is the Lead Planner and founder of K Sherrie + Company Planning Atelier, a full service wedding planning boutique for the discerning and style-conscious bride. She also operates a creative and inspiring wedding blog:* The Wedding Workroom. *After graduating from Danville High School, she studied Chemistry at Spelman College and went on to obtain her Doctor of Pharmacy at Butler University.*

So, how did she end up in the wedding industry? It was always in her blood! She planned parties and weddings of classmates and family while in pharmacy school, many times during class. She always stayed current on the fashion trends and new ideas in the wedding industry, so much so that one of her Therapeutics professors started calling her "Glamour Girl." She always had her head in some type of fashion or wedding glossy, alternating with Principles of Drug Action *textbooks. She planned her first full-service wedding from start to finish during clinical rotations. The couple she planned for was extremely pleased and that sealed the deal! After working 9 years in the pharmacy industry, Katasha has truly cultivated her skills for organization, expert planning and meticulous attention to detail. All things considered—at least the decisions that she now makes planning events can't potentially kill someone! Although formally educated in the areas of mathematics and science, she has always possessed an artistic flair, an eye for style and details, and a creative mind. After consistently being called upon to plan parties, organize professional benefits and fundraisers, and design weddings for friends and family after graduation, she began laying the groundwork to start her own boutique wedding planning firm in 2006. She went back to school, took some business classes, became a certified wedding planner and interned under a successful wedding planner in Indianapolis. Among other things, in the free time that she has left, Katasha enjoys mentoring young ladies as a Girl Scout Cadette troop leader and Alpha Kappa Alpha Sorority, Inc. Rosebud Mentor for Alpha Mu Omega Chapter. She also is a member of the Circle City Chapter of The Links, Inc. and serves on the Board of Directors for Girl Scouts of Central Indiana, United Way Youth As Resources and Shalom Health Care Center in Indianapolis.*

K Sherrie + Company Planning Atelier is a full service wedding planning firm. The best service that they offer is a stress-free planning experience for your special celebration. They save you time and ensure that you get the best possible services for your money. They are not here to make decisions for you, but to guide and assist you in making informed decisions. Their training, knowledge, expertise and experience allows them to take your dreams and execute them to your specifications. They want you to host an event designed to your personal aesthetic, where you kick back, relax and have a great time! Let them use their imagination and creativity to design an unforgettable party! They specialize in all encompassing full service planning and design to partial planning, down to our extensive "Month-Of" coordination. You should know that planning your wedding with K Sherrie + Company Planning

Atelier would be a luxury and couture planning experience with unparalleled service that produces a matchless event. Their websites include: www.ksherrieco.com, www.eventologyconference.com, and www.theweddingworkroom.com.

What advantages do you think you have as a single solo business owner that married people don't have?

TIME! Being single gives you time to work on all of the many facets of your business. As someone who takes marriage and family very seriously, I don't think I would be able to devote as much time as I would need to my company with a husband and/or children. As a current single person, time is still a precious commodity. You would have to have a very, very understanding spouse in order to make it work, but I don't necessarily think it would be fair.

What about disadvantages?

Lack of resources is a disadvantage. Because I have to eat, live, and take care of myself, it is not as easy for me to quit my day job (as a professional pharmacist) to pursue my business full-time. I'm not quite sure that I would even want to do that, but not having a spouse that could potentially take care of the household takes that decision off the table.

Do you think business ownership has led you to remain single?

No. But I think it causes me to self-select. I meet a higher caliber of people by virtue of being a business owner. Only men with a little more to offer stay in the running because they think I'm very driven.

Did you, or are you running your business as a part-time or full-time venture? Why?

It is a part-time venture, but the hours it takes to do it successfully are full-time!

Single. Women. Entrepreneurs.

What would it take for you to consider taking on your business full-time?

In order to take the business full-time, I would have to have a large enough stash that would support me at my current lifestyle AND I would need the business to be able to make at least the same income that I enjoy as a pharmacist. I would really need to put in more work and more hours to build up enough staff and clientele to reach that benchmark.

What advice would you give another single woman who is thinking about starting a business?

With careful planning, prayer and supplication—you can do it! There will be highs and lows, ebbs and flows, but it will all be worth it in the end if you are truly doing what makes you happy. Another added bonus: you become an inspiration for others! I did not plan to be a business owner to be an inspiration to other people, but it is really humbling to hear men and women tell you that you've inspired them.

What about being a single WOMAN business owner? Do you think it is easier, the same, or harder than being a single man starting a business?

I think it depends on the field that you are entering. Being a woman in the wedding planning industry has been good for me. Maybe I would have more street credibility if I was married—I don't know!

What was the best training you received to prepare you as a business owner?

The best training I received was, and is, networking with other wedding planner colleagues. Many people have traveled this road before me, and I can learn from their mistakes. Everything that I am doing, I didn't have to reinvent myself. During the first twelve months of my company, KSCo, I was a total sponge—learning all that I could from planners outside of Indianapolis.

By Erin Albert

BUT—you also must be a help to your colleagues. You can't always take, take, take—you have to give ideas as well. That was the founding principle for Eventology Conference that I produce annually for start-up wedding planners and other wedding vendors. Eventology is an intimate, collaborative and intensive business conference designed especially for wedding professionals that brings real-life, applicable marketing and business information to enhance their wedding business.

Did you take on a partner in your business at any time?

I do not have a partner. I think I would hire employees before I would ever take on a partner.

If you had to start another business, what have you learned that you might do differently—either about yourself, or about how to run a business in general?

In the next business that I want to start, I would probably have to get additional capital, as I would be offering products instead of cognitive services. That would involve more people (investors) in the business. I'm not sure if I would do other things differently—whatever mistakes or missteps I have faced have all been learning opportunities and a chance to do it better next time.

How important were mentors in your entrepreneurial career?

I didn't have a specific mentor when I opened the business, but I did work for women who were business owners while I was in pharmacy school. I carefully observed how one in particular ran her business. Susan was very meticulous, paid careful attention to detail and how her company was represented, and she was extremely successful. That had a major impact on me. I always pay attention to the small things, the branding of my company, and how my business is portrayed. I think this sets my company apart from others. Although it is a part-time venture, I present in a way that makes clients think it's the only thing that I do. I learned this from her.

Did you start your business with your own capital?

I started KSCo with my own capital. I did not try to obtain capital from others.

How important are your social and personal networks to the success of your business?

My social and personal networks are extremely important to the success of my business. No amount of marketing can do for me what word of mouth referrals can. People who intimately know me, my character, my style and how I operate are my best business ambassadors. They also give me the needed push when I am going through my ebbs and lows.

What is your personal definition of success, and have you achieved it?

Being happy with your life and what you're doing with it is my definition. It's not about things and accolades and perceived success—it's truly about being happy. Yes, a comfortable living helps with this, but I think there's more to it than money. It's the people you share your life with, the impact you have on others, and the way you steward what you have.

I am happy right now, but I have not achieved the pinnacle of my happiness. It's coming!

Joan E. Champagne

White and Champagne

Joan **Champagne** *is a 42-year-old SWPF with no children and no pets, but with two thriving plants. She currently lives in Fishers, Indiana, and was raised in Carmel, Indiana. Joan concentrates on family law and estate planning, and earned her B.S. in Business from the Kelley School of Business, and her Doctor of Jurisprudence from Indiana University School of Law—Indianapolis. She began her law career in the Marion County Prosecutor's Office in Indiana, and then went on to serve as counsel for UAW members and their families assisting them in estate planning, bankruptcy, divorce, guardianship, paternity, custody and child support services. She also returned to prosecuting in Jefferson and Switzerland Counties and then worked for a large insurance company prior to founding her own firm with partner, Tess White. She loves music, movies and eating out (but not cooking).*

White and Champagne is a law firm on the northeast side of Indianapolis, Indiana. The firm practices family law, personal injury law, criminal law, and general civil litigation. The website of the firm is: www.whiteandchampagne.com.

Single. Women. Entrepreneurs.

Could you describe your firm in one sentence?

It is a woman owned law practice providing simple answers and efficient resolutions to your legal issues.

What advantages do you think you have as a single solo business owner that married people don't have?

I think the biggest advantage I have is that my time is very flexible, and I can be available seven days a week, 24 hours a day, if necessary.

What about disadvantages?

See above.

Do you think business ownership has led you to remain single?

No, I didn't start my business until I was 40, and was single when I started. I don't think if I was still working for a firm that I would necessarily be married by now either.

What advice would you give another single woman who is thinking about starting a business?

Make sure you have (some) money saved, and make sure you have a game plan in case your business does not succeed.

How much money saved is enough, in your opinion?

I really think that in an ideal world, you should have enough money aside for your living expenses for 1 year. I had saved around nine months' of living expenses, but money was really tight in those last few months because it took about a year to finally get back to something close to my previous salary.

Do you think there are advantages/disadvantages to being a single business owner? Do you think it is harder, or easier?

The freedom is great, but not having a partner to rely upon financially during "lean" months is very stressful.

By Erin Albert

What about being a single WOMAN business owner?
Do you think it is easier, the same, or harder than being a
single man starting a business?

I don't think it is more difficult for a single woman to own a business than a single man or a married man. I think it is about the same.

What was the best training you received to prepare you as a
business owner?

I talked to several people in solo and small firms. Also, I have learned from both my successes and failures in my business. An example of a success for us was that we built our own website. That saved us a ton of money. As far as failure, we overspent on a logo, business cards and letterhead that we really didn't need. At the time, we didn't realize that spending $4,500 on our business materials was unnecessary and that we didn't have to use a big company to develop our logo. We could have hired a freelancer for much less. Also, we have no administrative help—no secretary, billing manager, or any office help, so we had to learn how to work around all the administrative issues. Most of all, we had to learn how to keep a careful eye on billing and accounts receivable and be vigilant about retainers. It is especially difficult to collect from clients who didn't get the result they wanted with their cases.

Did you, or are you running your business as a part-time or
full-time venture? Why?

Full-time—that's how the bills get paid!

Do you think having a business partner made it easier to start
your business?

It has made things easier; two heads are better than one.

If you had to start another business, what have you learned that you might do differently—either about yourself, or about how to run a business in general?

I would have saved more money prior to starting the business, and I would have networked more, especially during the first year. Networking is how I get most of my referrals.

How important were mentors in your entrepreneurial career?

Important. It is essential to have some "go to" people in your life. For example, I have a friend who is a solo practitioner in law and who was seminal in helping me learn how to market my firm, deal with client payment issues, attract more clients, even how to handle administrative help issues. She's been instrumental as a mentor to me for the nuts and bolts of running a business because she's been in practice much longer than me. I also seek out mentors in my area of practice in law. For example, I practice primarily family law, so I have a mentor who has been practicing family law much longer than I have, whom I can call upon when I have a question about that area of law. It's important to have another professional who can help me because my partner in the law firm works in a completely different area of law than I do. It's important to have people I can call upon who are experts in my practice area. Some have been very generous with their time, knowledge and resources.

Did you start your business with your own personal capital?

My law partner and I started our business with our own capital.

Why do you think more single/divorced and widowed women start more businesses than men in their respective categories, and does your theory match your own rationale for starting a business?

The flexibility and the income potential, and yes, this matches my own rationale.

By Erin Albert

What is your personal definition of success, and have you achieved it?

My personal definition of success is loving what I do on the "good" days, tolerating what I do on the "bad" days, and making enough money to pay the bills and put a little away for a rainy day. In general, I think I've achieved it.

What other advice or issues would you like to share that weren't asked?

The big factor for me has been the scariness of being an entrepreneur. Going back to my mentor with a solo practice who is very successful and having this conversation with her serves as a perfect example. I was talking to her about money one day and sharing that I was scared about the money issues associated with being a business owner. Some months you can make good money, and what if you have a bad month and just don't make enough? It is not like I have a Mr. Joan at home ready to help me out—it's just me. My mentor replied that she had been a solo practitioner for 15 years and that she too has been scared every day of her life and is still scared. She also shared that you just have to judge how long you are OK with being scared.

I'm still adjusting to this as a new entrepreneur—the fear. That was one good true blue thing while working for someone else: a regular paycheck, and the security that came with it. I had it for the first 40 years of my life. I'll do what I have to do. I've always been single and I've risen to the challenge. If I needed to get a second job, I could. If my company went under, I could go back to working for someone else, but I hope that's not the case anytime in the near future.

Michaela Conley, MA CSMS

HPCareer.net

Anyone who knows **Michaela Conley** knows she is a connector. She enjoys nothing more than putting people together to see what great things may come of it, and has been connecting people for as long as she can remember. Michaela is a native Hoosier who migrated to the D.C. metro area in the mid 1990s after a divorce while completing her master's program at Ball State. She moved with her two teen-aged kids to the east coast where she knew only two other people. She worked primarily as a consultant on several projects in D.C. and Baltimore while trying to figure out what she really wanted to do. She always loved computers, beginning with her first, a Commodore 64. Being in the D.C. area during the time of the Internet age was exciting. She became a member of the "Netpreneur Association," which was created for those doing business on the Internet.

Single. Women. Entrepreneurs.

*HPCareer.Net is the leading social media career platform delivering career opportunities real time to individuals and groups based on their interests and qualifications exclusively in the health promotion industry, since 1999. As technology has changed, HPCareer.Net became an ASP or an application service provider for membership organizations, publishers and credentialing bodies whose members/subscribers' career goals align with a health promotion industry focus. HPCareer.Net has always been a huge supporter of the professionalism of the industry. In recent years, the company began hosting weekly webinars with nationally and internationally recognized experts on topics important to professions in the field. All of the webinars are both free to attend live or access via archived recording. All webinars are continuing education eligible, which is how the company generates revenue to sustain what Michaela considers to be a needed service to fellow professionals and the industry. Internationally, HPCareer.Net has created **IDWellness.org** along with a group of leading experts in wellness around the world to facilitate resource sharing and collaboration. Everyone who works for HPCareer.Net works out of his or her own home, including Michaela.*

Please discuss why you started your business.

I saw a need for myself. The more I looked at it and thought about it, it became obvious to me (prior to the social web which exists now), there was no way for people to connect with each other and start conversations, so I started a company to connect people in health promotion with each other.

Although I grew up and was educated in Indiana, part of the reason why I moved from Indiana is that I'm visually impaired. Without a car, I don't have freedom. So, I moved to a location with ample public transportation to be independent and meet people rather than depend upon others for transportation. Interestingly, when I did live in Indiana, people I met never thought I was actually from Indiana. I'm not sure if that was a product of having to do things differently because of my vision.

There are a lot of people in Indiana who are first generation college students. My parents thought you went to high school, got a factory job, and got married—the end. I followed the rules for a while and then I figured out they were wrong. I had a little catching up to do, but I made up for it.

Also, when I divorced, I not only needed independence for logistical reasons, but I also needed to find a place where I could start over—literally and figuratively. I narrowed down my moving choices to Washington D.C., Minneapolis, or Seattle. Seattle was out because I'd have the world's biggest sinus headache nine months every year. Minnesota was great, but it was colder than Indiana. I knew two people in Washington D.C., so I ended up heading there. It was my opportunity to do what I wanted to do by relocating.

Honestly, I think I started my business out of pure necessity more than anything else.

What advantages do you think you have as a divorced solo business owner that married people don't have? What about disadvantages?

It was a huge advantage for me to be solo, because there was no one in my house, in my head, or anywhere else saying, "We can't afford this," or "Go get a job for a while." There was no one there in the beginning to talk me out of being a business owner. Certainly there can be relationships that are very supportive of what you want to do; the other person believes in you and in what you do. But, I've talked to a lot of people—married and singles with a significant other—who never get beyond talking about starting a business because the environment isn't conducive.

There are disadvantages too. It is very frustrating that the old stereotype that a man is very hard driving in business and aggressive and ambitious, but if a woman is, she's labeled as a bitch. Also, if you're quitting your day job in order to start your business full-time, you better have money in the bank or a husband or significant other who will support you. Going it alone can be a huge financial risk.

The other side of that is: if not now, when? For me, I just started my business. It was my single focus.

Single. Women. Entrepreneurs.

How do you define success?

A long time ago, a gentleman writing another book when I had just started my business interviewed me. I said if I could make $1,000 per month from this business I thought it would have been "successful." But it was some random measure. I couldn't see beyond something that seemed slightly realistic.

I think I would say that success to me now is having something to do every day that I can't wait to get down to my desk and start doing. Success changes over time, but success is being able to keep doing what it is that you want to do, create a sense of purpose for yourself, and be excited about what you do. Ultimately, I also like to say my long-term goal is to develop an evil plot to take over the world. It's not really evil—it's nice—but no one would take over a nice plot to take over the world. I started in 1996, and I'm still going.

Do you think business ownership has led you to getting remarried?

Being remarried now, I could never see myself with someone who didn't see what I do at least as important as what they do, and vice versa. They need to really be passionate about what they are doing and understand the passion I have for what I'm doing. Otherwise, it would just be an ongoing brewing argument. We got married in 1999. But, it was just me running the business for a long time. Then we started competing, and I started making more money than him in his job, so he decided to stay home and work with me.

How has it been working with your spouse in your business?

It's been a wonderful experience and continues to be; I attribute it to our close and supportive relationship. I'm lucky to be on a team with my very best friend. Our skill sets are very complementary in that I am more technical and creative with a "big picture" viewpoint, while he is more detail-oriented and all about the numbers.

By Erin Albert

What advice would you give another single woman who is thinking about starting a business?

Overall: whether it is spouse, parents, etc.—you've got to have and be in a place that is supportive. Otherwise, it just becomes too exhausting and unsustainable. You have to have someone who will share those little breakthroughs and not beat you up about the things that didn't work out.

Also, go to people who are doing what you want to do and find out how it is going for them. Ask them what they'd change. For example, in my field right now, there is a boom in health and wellness coaching. It seems like a really great idea (to be your own boss), but then there are a lot of business skills that you don't think about initially as important to run your own business. When people forget them, just go for it and start the business, they then shockingly realize that owning and running a business is not glamorous on a daily basis. For example, what system are you going to use for accounting? There are always more skills that you will need as an entrepreneur that are easy to forget. People also tell me that I'm lucky to have the opportunity to attend conferences. But just last week I was sitting in the airport in Milwaukee when the airport was shut down because of flooding. It is not always fun being a business owner.

Being an entrepreneur can also be very lonely. The time you must put into your business can really be enormous. You think about it a lot. There is so much thought and decision-making that goes into starting a business. Ideas on the business are always cooking in the back of your brain. Also, when the economy is bad, it is hard on business owners when business is slow. I had too much time on my hands last year during the really low point in the economy. It was really depressing because I was kind of used to a sort of flow in the business and it wasn't happening. It makes you feel out of control. That in turn can lead to the general conflict of structure. If you are used to structure, it can be a challenge to find structure in your own business. My significant other (now my husband) was in sales, which is very similar in this respect to business ownership, so he understood what I was going through at the time.

Single. Women. Entrepreneurs.

What was the best training you received to prepare you as a business owner?

I would say that it was more trial and error than any other type of training. There were tidbits here and there, but I don't really think there was one person or class that prepared me. It was a chain of events, paying attention, and assimilating bits and pieces from others.

For example, a guy I met at a networking function wrote the first version of the software for my company. I just told him what I was seeking and thinking about, and it ironically worked out that he would build it for me as part of development for his own portfolio. I was just at the right place at the right time, along with some luck and maybe some good karma thrown in too.

Now I get informal calls from people who really want to do something on their own. I'll spend some time on the phone with them and invite them to call me back and let me know how they are doing. It's like my elephant analogy: everyone is blind folded, but one person feels the tail of the elephant, another the backside, and another the trunk. It feels different for each of them, but it is the same elephant. Everybody comes to entrepreneurship from a different perspective. It is what it is, and in order to be successful you must keep your head down and keep going.

If you had to start another business, what have you learned that you might do differently—either about yourself, or about how to run a business in general?

I think I'd worry less about the details. In the past I had been very thorough and a little obsessed about all the details of owning and running a business—using the right accounting system as an example. I don't feel that way about customers, but in the end, the little stuff really doesn't make a difference.

What is your favorite thing about being a business owner?

If it occurs to me and I see a need, I just go fill it as a business owner, and I love that. I don't have to write a proposal, get someone else's approval, or get tangled up in bureaucratic BS—I just go do it.

By Erin Albert

What is your least favorite thing about being a business owner?

Someone not writing me a check is my least favorite thing. I can't always walk away at 5 p.m. either. I'm doing a webinar tonight at 8 p.m. because it is a different time in Australia. That's the bad part about being a business owner for me; I have to be available for the customer. Three months ago was the worst month ever for my business, but things are better now, because I spent the time working on developing the business. The best time to build is when times are bad—when we recover we will be dancing in the streets!

Anything else?

With every job I had in the past, when I got comfortable with it, I began to ask what other things we could try. The manager would always tell me, "That's not your job." I used to think something was really wrong with me because the job thing didn't work for me in that respect. This is counter-intuitive from what the professors tell you and what the books say. Even my parents told me to just go and get a job (even though my dad technically was a part-time entrepreneur). My family had the right intentions; they didn't want me to starve on the streets. But, the thing that I learned is that there are plenty of people out there doing their own thing and if you are of like mind and decide to join the ranks of the unemployable by being an entrepreneur, it is really OK. There wasn't anything wrong with my perspective after all. But who knew? "Go get that normal job and be normal, why don't you?" was what they kept telling me.

Fooled them!

Ann
Fisher, MS

HR Alternative Consulting, Inc.

Ann **Fisher, M.S.** *has a broad background in human resource management. She has multi-level, hands-on human resource experience and obtained major accomplishments throughout her career. Prior to establishing HR Alternative Consulting, Ann served as Vice President of Organizational Development for a multi-location hospital in the United States. Ann is founder and President of HR Alternative Consulting, Inc. Ann's education, professional certifications, and affiliations include: a M.S. degree from Purdue University in Industrial/Organizational Psychology, and a B.S. from the University of Washington in Psychology; and her business is certified as a women's business enterprise (WBE) with the city of Indianapolis and state of Indiana. She is also a member of the Society of Human Resource Management, a board member of the National Association of Women Business Owners, and a volunteer at Dress for Success.*

*****HR Alternative Consulting, Inc.** is a full-service human resource consulting firm. Their goal is to assist organizations and schools to* be PROACTIVE instead of REACTIVE by providing stand-alone human resource services, or consult with HR staff. They work to identify areas that need to be developed or improved, and then implement the right programs. You can find them on the web at www.hralternativeconsulting.com.

Ann is also Editor of HR News Magazine. As Owner and President of HR Alternative Consulting, Inc., she is continually being asked how other business owners and HR professionals handle common HR issues and concerns. How do businesses maintain compliance, and eliminate the potential of costly employee related lawsuits and yet, run their businesses or departments? HR News Magazine was created to provide information for those individuals dealing with the ever-changing HR federal and state laws. You can find the magazine at www.hrnewsmagazine.com.

Why did you start HR Alternative Consulting?

I started thinking about the idea of a business in 2002. I had been working as a vice president of organizational development for a hospital out of state. I was raised in Indiana. However, 9/11 happened and I moved back home to be closer to family. The job market was bad at that time. People were scared. Actually, my mother talked me into starting my own business. She told me, "You have a master's degree and years of experience in HR, so do something you love to do and start your own business," and so I did! In 2002, I spent the year researching the idea of a HR consulting company. I knew nothing about starting a business. I had to do a lot of research not only on how to start a business, but I also had to learn about the HR consulting market in Indianapolis. I even incorporated myself because I didn't have the funds to hire an attorney. I had no contacts, no clients, and had just moved back to Indianapolis. I started the business by incorporating officially in 2003.

What advantages do you think you have as a single business owner that perhaps married people don't have?

By Erin Albert

The first thing that comes to mind is that I have the flexibility to do what I need to do in order to run my business. I leave the house in the morning to attend networking events usually by 6:30 or 7 a.m., I'm usually gone all day, and sometimes I network again in the evening. I don't feel guilty about doing it because I don't have to worry about leaving someone at home. That's the biggest advantage I perceive. I do my own thing when I want, how I want.

What about disadvantages?

Well, I miss a second income. You are the only person making the car and mortgage payments as a single person and that is a challenge unless you are independently wealthy. In the past, I sometimes envied the women business owners who did have spouses who could help supplement their incomes. If I have a client who is slow in paying, I still have to pay my bills on time. You still have to take care of yourself, which can be an extra burden.

Do you think business ownership has led you to remain single?

I would have to say it has a lot to do with it. Running a business means you have to bring in the work, and then do the work. Since I'm a consultant business owner, I need to do both. There is a lot of time demand between the office work and client meeting time. I signed up for some of the dating network sites a while ago and thought it would be a good way to get out and meet single men. But, because of the demands of my business, when I'm done for the day, the LAST thing I want to do is get on the computer or get cleaned up and meet someone for coffee when it might not be a good match. I found that the dating sites were more work for me! Some of them were so petty as well—I'd come home and ask myself why I wasted a perfectly good Saturday evening to date a bum, when I would have much preferred staying home and watching a good movie. I declared that if I meet Mr. Perfect, I would meet him when I least expected.

What advice would you give another single woman who is thinking about starting a business?

It is important to have a reserve or savings account, or something she can fall back on if business is slow. Meet with other women entrepreneurs to utilize them as mentors. Don't get discouraged when things aren't looking like they're going the right direction; you have to stay positive and know things are going to work out. Be sure to bounce ideas off of someone.

What about being a single WOMAN business owner? Do you think it is easier, the same, or harder than being a single man starting a business?

It depends upon whom you are talking with at a company, but in some cases, it has been a disadvantage. Male business owners sometimes think I'm a dumb blonde, and try to take advantage of the situation. Also, a few other business owners in the past have approached me on partnership opportunities, and while it sometimes sounds great to begin with, they try to take advantage of the situation. I just don't let it happen. I have surprised a number of men with my savvy business sense too. I was a psychology major and that has served me well in dealing with potential clients. I've learned how to read them—the nonverbal communication—and I have a good sense of when someone thinks they're pulling something over on me.

But, I also have to say that being a woman has its advantages. In some cases I learned after the fact that a competitor of mine was bidding, the competitor was a male, and he felt intimidated by me. My business is certified as a women's business enterprise (WBE) and the males view that as a disadvantage for them, and feel somewhat threatened by it. I guess they feel threatened thinking that a male business owner would prefer to work with an attractive female professional, rather than another male.

Can you talk more about your WBE certification? How has that helped you and/or your business?

My business is certified with the city of Indianapolis and the state of Indiana. There is also a national WBE certification that women business owners can obtain. In HR consulting, it has not been a huge advantage to my business. However, it does help me with networking. I am invited to a lot of networking events for MBE (Minority Business Enterprise)/WBE certified businesses and it opens the door for a lot of good networking with potential clients. In that way, it's helped me to open the door to get into different events. I thought about the national WBE certification, but federal business wants the cheapest HR rates possible, and I don't sell mass templates. I like to do custom work and do it specifically for clients. I'm not the cheapest HR consultant in town, either. You get what you pay for.

What was the best training you received to prepare you as a business owner?

This goes back in my personal history. My ex-husband owned his own business. We got married in Indianapolis and 2 days later moved to Seattle for his new job. A year later, he along with a few colleagues left and started their own consulting business. It actually turned me against entrepreneurs. I had to start asking him—can we make the mortgage payment? I was used to the regular paycheck and regular insurance; I knew where the money was coming from and when it was coming. That was the hardest thing for me to get used to—my husband owning a business—and honestly, that was part of the reason why we divorced. At one point in time, I swore I'd never be involved with or start my own business! Twenty years later, I now own a business. However, after returning to Indiana and seeing the job market, I also found there was a need and an opportunity with my skills and what I could offer to the community. Businesses and schools needed HR help, but many of them were not large enough to support a full-time HR professional. Instead, we could be their outsourced HR department!

Did you, or are you running your business as a part-time or full-time venture? Why?

It is full-time. For a while, I thought I was a full-time *networker*. I think I had one project the first year I started my business. To start, I attended each and every networking event I could find. In addition, I never had a finite timeline for trying out the business before I'd quit and go back to a day job. I simply decided this was the avenue I wanted to go for myself and I just stuck with it and knew it was going to get better because there was a need; it was just finding the right businesses to get in front of and understand what I could do to help them.

Did you take on a partner in your business at any time?

Over the years, I've had numerous individuals approach me about forming a partnership. When I first started attending the National Association for Women Business Owners (NAWBO) meetings, one of the members made a comment to me that has always stuck with me: she and a partner parted ways. She told me, "Never bring on a business partner." Since then, when I've been approached, I realized that I can do this work on my own and don't need any additional headaches. I don't want to have to go to a partner to get decisions approved. I'm also very independent and stubborn, so I can't say I've ever seriously considered taking on a partner.

If you had to start another business, what have you learned that you might do differently—either about yourself, or about how to run a business in general?

Actually, I just started another business! I am now editor of *HR News Magazine* (www.hrnewsmagazine.com). It is an internet based HR magazine. As editor, I talk to business owners and ask them how they handle basic HR issues. This provides insight to other business owners, and gives them guidance on how other busy business owners are handling specific situations. It is a free resource.

There is only so much time in a day, but I thought that developing this resource would be helpful to potential clients. So, I meet with and interview business owners. I have the interviews transcribed and then I hand the transcription over to an IT person who sets it up on the website. My time is spent getting in the door and talking to business owners, conducting the interviews and then passing off the information to other people who make it happen.

On the HR consulting side, I do not have W2 employees; I don't want them. I'm the expert. I know the kind of issues business owners run into and I don't want to worry about the expenses of an office and keeping other people busy for 40 hours a week. Typically, I outsource the work to other junior or senior HR people and pay them as a 1099. Originally, I took care of everything, but sometimes now that I know who to trust, I hire extra help. The 1099 tipping point for me was the roller coaster of networking, bringing in business and then sitting in front of the computer on nights and weekends to finish the work. I realized that I could hire help to assist me with the project work end, and I could still bring in the business on my own.

Do you have a business coach?

I do now. Originally, when I started my business, I was relying on other business owners and friends to vent and share my frustrations. I also got to a point in my business where I had done everything I could think of to grow my business, but didn't know how to move forward. I realized I was being a burden to my friends. Also, I needed someone to bounce ideas off and smack me in the face and tell me to get out of my own way. I had taken an on-line and conference call course from J.Sewell Perkins, founder of the Success Coaches Institute. Then, as I had completed a couple of her courses, I reached out and asked her how to grow my business. She is now my personal and business coach. To me, business and life tie together. If things aren't going well for me personally, they can also affect my business negatively. It is important to bounce ideas off someone who is not my friend. She sets the record straight and holds me personally accountable.

Did you start your business with your own capital?

It was my own capital. All I needed to start the business was a computer, internet access, and printer. You've got to have some money in the bank. I didn't want to get into debt not knowing how long it was going to take me to bring in clients and make money.

Why do you think more single/divorced and widowed women start more businesses than men in their respective categories, and does your theory match your own rationale for starting a business?

I think that more single women start their own business because they cannot find a good paying job in the workplace. I think we are very creative creatures and we've got good heads on our shoulders, so why not have women own businesses? We've taken care of homes, families and husbands, and while running a business is somewhat different, the same skills are involved—multitasking, budgeting, making decisions are all involved. I have a lot of good ideas, and working in corporate America where the bosses always had the final say was not always correct, especially in dealing with HR discrimination and inconsistencies in the workplace. I saw things that were happening in businesses operated by men that were not ethical or legal. I wanted to make a difference. When I go in as a consultant, they listen because they know I'm the expert.

What is your personal definition of success, and have you achieved it?

I think my definition of success for my business will happen when I find my clients coming to me, rather than me just out beating the bushes to find them. Also, I want to be happy with what I'm producing for clients, and knowing they are happy with the services I provide to them. Do I feel I've achieved it? Not yet. I think this will be the continuous struggle while I own my business. I keep striving to do better, make more money, and be a better person in the community. I don't think I'll ever feel satisfied with my definition of "success."

What didn't I ask you about you and your business that you wanted me to?

By Erin Albert

I'm very passionate about helping companies and schools get rid of their pain. Schools have had a lot of budget cuts. They are really struggling. I've actually cut my fees to go in and assist them. They really want to do the right thing for their staffs, and they don't want to lose funds for student programs. I'm more passionate about working with the schools because the budgets are limited and the last thing they want is a discrimination lawsuit, which might cost them funding for student programs. If I can keep their costs down, they don't have to hire a full-time HR professional, and they can still function properly without discrimination, harassment or other issues from their employees. Both of my parents were educators. My dad was a superintendant and mother was a teacher. I swore I'd never work for schools, but now, I have a real passion for helping schools.

Elizabeth Garber

The Best Chocolate in Town

Elizabeth Garber *grew up in Columbus, Indiana, with two older brothers and a twin sister. They vacationed in Michigan every summer, which is partly why she searched for a college to attend in Michigan. She attended Alma College and graduated with a B.A. in Art & Design. She remains involved in the arts by supporting local artists and cultural groups and still works in her own studio at home as time permits. She spends most of her time outside of work with her husband enjoying life. Cooking, gardening, reading and eating good food are her hobbies.*

The Best Chocolate in Town is Elizabeth's business, founded in 1998. Her first shop was located in Edinburgh, Indiana. After 1 year, she had to expand, so she moved north to Franklin, Indiana where she stayed for 7 years. After 8 years in the wholesale business, Elizabeth moved the company to Indianapolis, Indiana and opened a retail shop where it has been successful for the past 4 years and continues to grow. You can visit her shop online at: www.bestchocolateintown.com.

Single. Women. Entrepreneurs.

How did your pre-college graduation experiences play into starting your business?

My business began as a part-time venture when I was a senior in college—Elizabeth's Homemade Heavenly Dipped Candies. I started it because I needed to make some extra money as a college student. I figured that I could sell chocolate during the holidays. While my degree is in art and design, I also had minors in psychology and Spanish from Alma College in Michigan.

Growing up in Indiana, I chose to attend school far enough from home to be surrounded by a completely new environment, but still be close enough to home to visit during my college career. I knew I could do anything I wanted, and my goal was to get away and try something new and different. However, I planned on elementary education. My mom was a teacher, and it seemed like a good profession, until I met a guy in the quad next to me who was an art major. After watching him work, I went to a professor in the art department and switched to art and design as a major, because it was something different and interesting to me. My degree has been enormously valuable to me as a business owner. In the beginning, I created the design of the products, the size, style, and the packaging.

During the summer months of my college years, I worked at a camp. That experience formed a very solid foundation for group dynamics and participation, which is the same foundation upon which I now I run my company. My employees don't have "titles," and we have a fundamental philosophy of the business being a team effort. We currently have three full-time employees, five part-time employees, myself, and during the holidays we hire holiday temporary help as well.

Your mom was a teacher, but was your family entrepreneurial?

My dad is an attorney in private practice. He started his own firm. He worked for other companies before venturing out on his own. So yes, I'd call my dad fairly entrepreneurial. My mom being a teacher does not appear very entrepreneurial, but I definitely inherited my cheery, bubbly side from my mom. Now, my maternal grandparents were very entrepreneurial. They started a diner in 1929 and ran it until 1959 in Muskegon, Michigan.

What made you move from part-time to full-time in your business?

I continued to create and sell chocolate during the holidays after graduation, and also worked in an art gallery after I graduated. As I was working in the gallery full-time, I was still developing my chocolate business part-time and selling chocolate through a business owner in Nashville, IN. Her business with me exploded, so during the day I would continue to work in the gallery and then at night create chocolate for her.

It got to the point that I wasn't loving my gallery job, but loved the chocolate business; it was challenging, fun, and I felt like I could figure out how to make a living on this business. So, when I was 24, I actually quit my gallery day job and started my company—kind of the opposite of most people—wholesale only and retail only via a website, with no physical store front. The reason why I started this way was mainly money. I didn't have to pay loads of overhead cost in a high-traffic storefront and the website wasn't terribly expensive.

I found a commercial kitchen in 1998 in downtown Edinburgh, IN for $200 per month. I still had to do a lot of work to get it up to health department standards, but I did it and then moved my business from my home to the kitchen in Edinburgh.

Why chocolate as your business? (Not that we are complaining!)

Because I love chocolate and sweets! I have great memories of baking cookies with my grandmother during the holidays, but didn't want to have a cookie business. Chocolate was something different, a challenge, and at the time, was a really unique trade. Uniqueness is a key to running any business.

As a single woman and recent college graduate, what secret(s) did you have to making your full-time business a success?

Well, cash is king to a business owner, and I had to live on a credit line at one point. I lived (and still live) very frugally. For example, my favorite dinner then and now is pasta with garlic, olive oil, onions and Roma tomatoes. I'm not really into having 'stuff' either. I lived with someone for a while and we pooled our resources, which at the time seemed like a smart thing to do, although now I'm not sure I would recommend that.

Also, I rarely, if ever, took a day off for 3 years. I loved running and expanding my business, and would have worked Christmas day if my mom had told me not to work. At the time I started my business, I figured the worst that could happen to me was that I would have to close the business and go get another day job.

Now, I have more to worry about with full and part-time employees. I view my business as helping them pay their bills; they are relying on their hours and paychecks. It definitely adds pressure. But I think it is a responsibility to consider in making your business successful. Employees are an important asset to any business.

What does success mean to you?

I think my personal definition of success has changed over time. When I first started my business full-time, I measured success by the thrill of how many people were buying my products, and that people loved my product! This was really important to me. Then, while I was growing the business, success then became attaining our break even numbers, then making a profit. But, I also had to put more money into inventory and growing the business as well, and that was a challenging balance for me. At years three, five and seven in particular, I had bigger financial challenges. At years five and seven, I asked myself—shouldn't I be making more money? At year seven, I decided that I had two choices: either move the business to a retail space and fully expand into retail, or close the business altogether. I took the first path. The chocolate industry was changing and it was becoming much more difficult to sustain only a wholesale business. Now, I have both wholesale and retail businesses and they are growing.

By Erin Albert

The meaning of success has changed for me over time. At first, selling meant success, then break-evens meant success, and then profits meant success. Right now, success is continually growing my business while making a profit and having time to spend with my family.

You were single when you started your business. What advantages do you think you had by being a single business owner?

From 1998-2006, I was single. Then, in 2006, I got married, moved the business and moved into a house with my husband, and he took a new job all in the same year. Although that was a lot of stress on both of us, my husband brought me the gift of more balance. When I was single, it was all about me, and I could spend all the time I wanted at the business (which I view as an advantage). When I was married, I wanted to spend more time with my husband, and found balance through hiring more employees and giving up some level of control.

Balance is a big sticky point with women. What is your definition of balance, and do you really think it can be achieved?

Balance is whatever makes you happy. The amount of time you spend at your company isn't seemingly balanced to the external world, but it can be balanced for you if that is what you want. To me, being single and working a lot of hours was balance. Balance can really be customized.

Now that I'm married, my custom definition of balance is different. I figured out how to work on tasks that I wanted to and found employees who could do tasks that I didn't like to do. I also don't need to be at the business on weekends. I can be gone when I want to be and it works well for my own "balance" now. Even payroll, which I know how to do, I'm handing off to an outside vendor so I can spend my time focusing on other parts of the business.

What was the toughest lesson for you to learn as a manager?

My toughest lesson learning to be a good manager was allowing my employees to make mistakes. Many ideas or methods that my employees think of, I've thought of already, just by nature of the experience factor and using a particular material. I often let them make the mistake themselves and learn from it, even if I know it won't work. If it is an expensive mistake, I don't let them make it. But constantly telling your employees, "no," or that something won't work without letting them have a crack at it isn't helpful to their work experience. We all learn by making mistakes. Some of those mistakes lead us into great innovation. Someone once said that experience is much more valuable than how many degrees you have, and I find that to be so true.

If you had to start another business, what have you learned that you might do differently, either about yourself, or how to run a business in general?

I would now plan differently. I would be more money focused in the beginning by creating better cash flow. Cash is king to a small business.

If you met a young woman who was thinking of starting a business, what advice would you have for her?

Go through the experience of writing the business plan. It is hard! Where do you think you'll be in 5 years? How many customers will you obtain during the first year? The second year? These questions are sometimes difficult to answer, but it is worth struggling with it. Granted, there are so many unpredictable things like relationships and the economy, which are difficult to forecast. But, think some scenarios through—things like equipment you'll need, estimate sales, find your potential competitors, and guesstimate. I found my original business plan goals are still on target. Whatever it is you want to do, write it down.

Continue learning. My education is still continuing. Even though I don't have a M.B.A., I'm reading a ton of books on marketing, branding, and other tasks relative to owning and running a business. I'm always an advocate for education. It can only help to better prepare you for business and hopefully prevent mistakes along the way that could cost you your business.

If you are single, think long and hard about your personal lifestyle before starting a business. How much money do you need and want to live on? Are you ready to give up the $5 a day on Starbucks? If you can't afford something, are you going to be OK with that? Is the business you want to create going to be expensive? How much do you have in savings, and are you willing to lose it all? Do you have a backup plan for your life? Your house? Your bills?

If you are a single parent, remember that starting a business will not only affect you, but also your kids. If you are fully aware of the absolute worst-case scenario and you can still deal with that situation, then go for it! Just be careful of setting your own expectations—make sure they are realistic and you can find joy on the other side of them. Know yourself. Do all the personality tests you can to fully understand your strengths. You'll need to know what your holes, gaps, or weaknesses are too.

Lastly, you have to be flexible and go with the flow when you start your business. Plan multiple scenarios. Always be prepared, and be ready to change if you need to.

Lynn Griffith

Welcome Events

S tarting her business career with a degree in linguistics and having fluency in French, Spanish, and English, **Lynn Griffith** followed a path into the travel and tourism industry. After experimenting as a tour guide and travel director, she discovered a perfect opportunity in Florida. As the nation's number one incentive and meeting destination, and with a very limited number of quality providers of event management services, Lynn opened her first company in 1984 to service corporate America in the Florida marketplace. As her business grew, they added services such as bringing all décor services and teambuilding services in-house. Lynn then grew her business outside of the Florida marketplace. As she built her business, she certified it as a WBE (women's business enterprise) through the Women's Business Enterprise National Council (WBENC) certification program. She has been very involved in this organization and through WBENC, has helped to build the recognition of the certification and the professionalism of women in business. Lynn serves on various Boards of Directors in the diversity *and women owned business realm, and is passionate about mentoring and helping women start and grow their businesses.*

Welcome Events has been in business for 27 years, and provides event management and logistics expertise to corporate America. They are an event planning company offering teambuilding events, themed events, décor, entertainment, transportation services, tours and activities and hotel selection to corporations for sales meetings, incentive programs, and product launches. From handling the logistics program for the 1996 Olympic Torch Relay for the company's client, The Coca-Cola Company, to providing the décor for the celebration party for the Indianapolis Colts after winning the Super Bowl, they offer innovative and creative programming to achieve their clients' goals. The company website is www.welcomeevents.com.

What advantages do you think you have as a solo business owner that married people don't have?

Being alone provides the time to focus the intensive amount of energy it requires to build a business, without distractions, and without having to focus on your partner's needs or challenges.

What about disadvantages?

Conversely, although you do not have the distraction of a spouse's emotional requirements, there is also no one available in that key position to share your successes and achievements.

Do you think business ownership has led you to remain single after your husband passed?

Somehow, I was able to fall in love and marry 8 years into owning my own business. I do believe that keeping our marriage fresh and alive was more challenging than if I had had a "normal job." Two years ago as my husband became terminally ill, it was my business and the ability to throw myself fully into my business as a distraction that pulled me through the great sadness that encompassed me through his illness and after his passing.

By Erin Albert

They say entrepreneurs attract other entrepreneurs—did you?

I married my husband 8 years into my business. He was NOT an entrepreneur and it took him a very long time to understand that side of me. Our relationship was very odd. When our daughter was born, he became "Mr. Mom" and I remained the primary income earner. Later, he joined my business. Although he was truly my partner in life, he very much functioned as an employee in the business and that relationship had many, many challenges. To him, it was a job and that was very difficult for me to understand since it was, always, my passion.

What advice would you give another single woman who is thinking about starting a business?

My first reaction to this question is DO IT. I would never try to discourage anyone from chasing his or her dream. I would, however, caution anyone considering starting a business to make sure that they are prepared for the price to be paid. Building your own business extracts a high emotional price. It will, and should, become your obsession, your best friend, your source of reassurance and satisfaction. You will become so immersed in it that it is easy to neglect friends, family, and most of all yourself. There is much to be said for work/life balance and this is truly a feat to accomplish when you are an entrepreneur. DO NOT neglect yourself and DO NOT marry your business. Both of these are mistakes I made in my first business.

Do you think there are advantages/disadvantages to being a single business owner? Do you think it is harder, or easier?

I was single for the first 8 years of my first business. I am widowed now as I open my next business and begin to build it. It is both easier and harder to be single as I enter this adventure.

It is easier since your time is your own and you can create that laser focus on your business with few distractions. A new business is truly like a new baby and must be held and cuddled and tended to constantly and with much care and love. It requires an incredible amount of both your time and your complete attention.

Single. Women. Entrepreneurs.

It is harder for multiple reasons. To experience a husband with an independent income would certainly have reduced the stress of making the new business support me very quickly. It also is an advantage to have that sounding board at home every night waiting to hear of your day's challenges and willing to give strong and loving support and advice. The feeling of loneliness I have had building both businesses was acute.

What about being a single WOMAN business owner? Do you think it is easier, the same, or harder than being a single man starting a business?

Although I think the country has made many advances in equality for men and women, I think there are still additional challenges for women. I have had male sales managers for the past 10 years, primarily because I have seen the difference in the way customers respond and react to men versus women. Regardless of product knowledge, personal style and sales ability, I believe that the male businessmen are just taken more seriously. I have had many people say that I "think like a man." I think this is very true. It is an ability that I developed early on. I have consciously suppressed my femininity and deepened my voice in order to be taken more seriously by both customers and suppliers. In addition to being a woman, I am also barely 5 feet tall, so the challenge to be taken seriously in the business world is even more challenging on first impression.

What was the best training you received to prepare you as a business owner?

This is probably not the answer you are expecting. I knew that I was an entrepreneur when I was fired from the tenth job in 2 years. I had total intolerance working for people who I either did not respect or did not have the knowledge and ability that I felt I had. I could not seem to conform to the responsibilities of being an employee. The "training" received was in seeing that I clearly understood that I was not "employee material" and my only option was to blaze my own trail.

By Erin Albert

Did you, or are you running your business as a part-time or full-time venture? Why?

Full-time. My business both requires and deserves my full-time attention. Since I am so passionate and focused on building my business, I cannot imagine it any other way.

Did you take on a partner in your business at any time?

I never had a partner in business. However, with the new business that I am launching, I am seriously considering a partner. She is also a woman and has a very different skill set than mine. She could offer both the talents of the position she would fill and the camaraderie of a partner. I have to admit after my laser sharp focus alone on my initial business for over 25 years, I do feel the need to spend a little more time "smelling the roses" and I believe that a partner could provide the support to allow me more free time for that pursuit.

Can you share with us more about what your new business will be? Do you view yourself as a serial entrepreneur?

I was in business for several years before I even knew what an entrepreneur was and that it was a completely accurate description of me. Prior to that, I always looked at myself as someone who owned my own business. I believe that there is a real difference between a business owner and an entrepreneur. Sometimes I even believe that there is an "entrepreneurial gene." I came to it so naturally! And once I discovered entrepreneurship, it explained many of my job failures and dissatisfactions very clearly. Any entrepreneur is by nature a "serial entrepreneur" and will most likely start additional businesses depending on necessity and the right situation arising. When our economy stumbled so badly a few years ago, one of the most injured industries was the meeting and event industry. Not only did it suffer from those financial challenges, but also the "bad rap" of the junkets and meetings as being "frivolous." We received over 4 million dollars in cancellations within two months and almost without exception they were companies with financial stability; companies that merely didn't want to be perceived as spending unnecessary money at "resorts" or on "trips" and "meetings."

What a wakeup call that was, and I immediately set to assessing my skills, observing the marketplace and determining what other business options might be out there for me. "Getting a job" as my business declined rapidly in volume was never an option that I considered. My new business, "WELCOME WALKS" takes advantage of a talent that I have developed over the 25 years with WELCOME EVENTS. That is the ability to script tours. It also will benefit from my extensive client base and contacts throughout the United States. I have blended the "green" movements, elements of physical fitness, and the rapid advancement of technology into a company that offers downloadable walking tours. No paper, no gas from buses on tours, no waste at all. To take my tours, you will need to put on your walking shoes and get outside in the fresh air as you exercise and learn. And you can download my tours directly to your latest gadget—be it a MP3 player, smartphone, or iPad®. I plan on launching this business online by the end of 2010 with the first 25 cities. An additional 25 cities will come on line within the following six months. My future plans include adding European and Asian tours to our inventory, as well as translating our various U.S. tours into additional languages.

As with my first business, I think this one will take a lot of hard work and passion, blended with a little luck and a bit of magic.

How important were mentors in your entrepreneurial career?

I had no mentors. I wish I had. I try very hard at this point in my career to mentor other women entrepreneurs.

Did you start your business with your own capital?

The story of starting my business is very unique, I think, and very funny. I started my business with no money at all. I had no business education and very little business savvy. I stumbled on a service that I excelled in. There was also a bit of serendipity since I was definitely in the right place at the right time. I had 14 checking accounts going in my first year (one for every client account). I waited until all of the bills were paid from each account, leaving my profit. I would then transfer the balance into the company checking account. Very early on, my phone was cut off for non-payment because I did not understand the concept of cash flow and putting all clients' deposits into one account and using that money to pay bills. How much I have learned and how far I have come fascinates me, because I can remember that experience as if it were yesterday.

How important are your social and personal networks to the success of your business?

I am not sure that I actually have a social or personal network. I started my business long before the internet or social networking. My business network consists of 27 years of suppliers, colleagues, clients, and industry acquaintances. They are supremely important and these relationships are crucial to the ongoing success of my business.

Why do you think more single/divorced and widowed women start more businesses than men in their respective categories, and does your theory match your own rationale for starting a business?

I would guess that if there are more divorced and widowed women starting more businesses than men, it is probably a question of necessity. I don't think that women are more entrepreneurial. Divorced and widowed women probably have children and a greater need to make a living. For those single mothers, there is more time flexibility to self-employment, particularly the option of home-based businesses.

The need to support a family was not a rationale for me. It was simply the need to both support myself and do something that I enjoyed, which drove me to self-employment.

What is your personal definition of success, and have you achieved it?

My definition of success is the profound sense of pleasure and contentment that comes when you have reached financial stability, achieved personal milestones, and attained the respect and confidence of clients and peers. It is a self-satisfaction that comes from knowing that you have "arrived!"

What other single women business owners do you admire, and why?
I admire all single women business owners. They are a different breed than married business owners, since they have achieved their successes solo.

How do you and did you make key decisions on growing or shifting your business?
Trust your gut. I think a crucial characteristic in any woman's tool belt are her instincts. The ability to trust your instincts and act quickly and decisively almost guarantees success in your business.

Dava Guthmiller

Noise 13 Design

Dava Guthmiller *is the owner/creative director of Noise 13 Design (noise13.com). Since 2000, this branding and design firm has worked with business to consumer lifestyle companies in order to create memorable brands that connect the company story to the end users. Dava earned her B.S. degree at Academy of Art University, where she also spent 2 years as an instructor. Dava also started a networking group for savvy women in business in 2004 called Pow.wow Network (powwownetwork.org and @powwownet on Twitter). This group meets monthly to share ideas, get peer feedback, and learn from each other. To expand on her passion for food and explore in more detail the policies and politics that push the food and beverage industries she deals with for branding, Dava is also involved in the non-profit, Slow Food. Currently the San Francisco Chapter president (slowfoodsanfrancisco.com, @SlowFoodSF on Twitter), she works to expand the ideals of good, clean and fair food. Dava is also a member of AIGA, the Designers Accord, and a winner of the*

2010 Make Mine a Million $ Business Competition. You can reach her though the Noise 13 website above, by email (dava@noise13. com), by phone (415) 957-1313, on Twitter (@Noise13Design) or LinkedIn.

*About **Noise 13 Design**: Your brand makes your business. Their business makes your brand. An organization's success is determined by the power of its message, and its ability to communicate that message in a meaningful, appropriate way. Noise 13 Design works with businesses to define captivating brands that reflect their goals and distinguish them within the marketplace. Since their beginning, in January of 2000, Noise 13's work has been featured in* HOW, Print, Communication Arts, Architecture, 7x7, Edible, *and* San Francisco *magazines, and has won many awards and accolades.*

Can you please describe your business in one sentence?

Noise 13 is a full service branding and graphic design firm specializing in life style brands and industries.

What advantages and disadvantages do you think you have as a single solo business owner that married people don't have?

I think the biggest advantages are freedom in my schedule, and the ability to travel on short notice. I don't really see any major disadvantages as a single woman business owner. You do need mental support in running a business. So if you don't have it at home from a partner, or friend who knows business, then get a business coach. Releasing frustrations, and thinking through ideas are better with someone to work with.

Do you think business ownership has led you to remain single?

I've been in business for 11 years, since January of 2000, and I definitely think it has lead me to remain single much longer because of my time commitment to my business versus dating and having children.

By Erin Albert

Is your current significant other an entrepreneur?

No.

What advice would you give another single woman who is thinking about starting a business?

Make sure you maintain balance between your business and personal life. Also, learn how to delegate. Ask for help. Hire people to do the work you aren't good at and/or don't like to do.

What about being a single WOMAN business owner? Have you perceived any advantages or disadvantages to being a woman business owner?

I see two disadvantages for women: 1. They don't ask for help enough and 2. They definitely feel as though they have to prove themselves. Women think they HAVE to do it all; it is not trusting people to do as good as job as you. In terms of advantages, I think women have a different level of personal service inherent from our female traits of wanting to care for others. For example, in my business, we don't take on clients who we don't believe in and/or who have products that we don't love. I do not want to cover up a bad product or brand with good marketing, messaging or design. Women tend to be more caring and try to do it all; it is both a blessing and a curse. I think women just have to watch the balance in their lives as business owners.

Let's talk about balance, because that seems to be a subjective term. What does balance mean to you?

For me, balance means that however many hours you spend on your business, make sure you're also taking time for yourself, your health—both physical and mental—in order to achieve it. That means maybe taking weekends off, or going on vacation, or doing a hobby that you love. If all you do is work, you get caught up in the "work is you" problem; you tend to lose yourself in your job. I've done that. The balance between your work and doing things that you love but are not your job are really important.

Single. Women. Entrepreneurs.

What was the best training you received to prepare you as a business owner?

Actually, it was working as an employee for another company where I was given the opportunity to pretty much run the business. I had hands on training in that particular situation. In school, I can't say I had much training on how to be a business owner. School was great for creativity, but I learned absolutely nothing in school that taught me how to run a business. I grew up in a family run business and being in that atmosphere was extraordinarily helpful. I had the chance to be around the family business from a young age, and then grew up, learned and did bookkeeping and accounting in the family business.

Did you, or are you running your business as a part-time or full-time venture?

Full-time. I basically came back from vacation, quit my job, freelanced for a couple of months, and then incorporated. It was time to quit my job. I was actually thinking of leaving before my vacation. I had a freelance client and my day job was just not as collaborative an environment as I would have liked to work within. I actually returned from my vacation, and had a major disagreement with my boss and decided it was time for me to leave.

Growing up in a family business, was entrepreneurship something you always considered, or was it an instant idea?

Entrepreneurship was and is always something I thought about; I just wasn't exactly sure what type of business I wanted. I contemplated several different business ideas—opening a restaurant/café, graphic design, or consulting were my choices. It was definitely something I always wanted to do. The two biggest reasons why I wanted to be a business owner were: 1. I knew I could do it, and 2. I really wanted to create a more collaborative environment to work within, rather than the top down model. My office is definitely very open book, and a lot of people who work for me either freelanced in the past or went on to manage teams.

By Erin Albert

Did you take on a partner in your business at any time?

I did. I had a business partner for the first year of my business, in 2000, and honestly, he did not want to work as hard as I did, so I bought him out at the beginning of 2001. I would still consider taking on a partner, and I've considered it even recently, if I could find someone who has corporate business experience and new media experience. I've got more experience in print and strategy, so it would be great to have a partner who had more expertise in other areas. I have to rely on my team now to get new media done for clients. So, I would still consider a partnership at this point.

If you had to start another business, what have you learned that you might do differently—either about yourself, or about how to run a business in general?

I would definitely ask for help earlier. I would also write a business plan; I never did that. It would be good to clearly identify goals before you start a business, rather than just running it out of necessity and on passion. Also, I think now I would be able to more quickly fire clients if they just aren't the right fit.

Who are your ideal clients?

Our service is a very personal one, because it is conveying what a company is to the public, and that is very personal to smaller start up companies. If we have a new client and they've never worked with a graphic design team before, they must be open to collaboration and understand what brand, design and marketing can do for their business. If they don't value that, then they don't really value what we are doing for them. We aren't here just to take their money. We also focus on business to the consumer, and we are lifestyle oriented. In the past, the company might take on assignments just because the client had cash, and the project might not be a great fit for our company. But now, we are spending a lot of time up front to figure out if we are a good fit for the client. Sometimes, we only work with a client for a month, but most we have a long term working relationship with, over 5-10 years. It's a lot like dating: if you don't get along and there's a lot of stress and strain, you shouldn't move in together.

How important were mentors in your entrepreneurial career?

Huge. I had some amazing teachers when I was in college who were very supportive and provided the viewpoint of what it's like to be out on your own. I did have other friends who owned businesses who were supportive. I actually even started a women's networking group because I needed to know how to hire people and started meeting with a group of women business owners in order to get that feedback, advice and help. That group, Pow.Wow Network (www.powwownetwork.org) has been around for 8 years. It has been a super supportive network of women. When I first started it, there was really nothing in the creative industries like it; most women's networking organizations were white-collar women who wore suits and were in banking and real estate. Over the years, we have accumulated women in every industry in our group, but it is also a supportive learning environment, rather than hardcore networking and distribution of business cards. We now have over 400 women on our email list. I also continue to seek support and mentoring through the Count me In/Make Mine a Million $ Business network. (www.makemineamillion.org). I am proud to say I am a 2010 M3 award winner as well.

Did you start your business with your own capital?

I just used my own capital since I freelanced. That, and a credit card because I had good credit. We have a line of credit for the business now, and I probably need to look into obtaining a SBA loan, but we haven't done that yet.

How important are your social and personal networks to the success of your business?

HUGE. I am a big networker, and 80% of our work is word of mouth referrals, networking or internal clients. We don't do marketing for ourselves either. So, if I stay home for two months and don't network, we have less business in the coming months. I also do events, help run a local non-profit, Slow Food San Francisco, (www.slowfoodsanfrancisco.com) and run Pow.Wow, and all allow me to constantly meet new people and expand our network. My Facebook, LinkedIn and Twitter accounts are huge in the social media era too.

Why do you think more single/divorced and widowed women start more businesses than men in their respective categories?

I think women who are solo discover that they have much more time on their hands, and are much more willing to be spontaneous. When you are single or recently divorced, you find out that you have a lot of free time, so you can either become super active in your personal life, or community, or start a business because you can focus on it with your time. Also, women (in general) start a business because they want to solve a problem or fix a frustration. For example, I didn't like the way my boss ran a business where I worked, so I quit and started my own business where I could control the culture and create a much more collaborative environment. I can fix the problem, and how I do that is through creating the environment where I work by creating my own job. For other women, maybe they are tired of resting their purses on the floor, so they create some type of hook to address and fix that problem. It's not necessarily about the money for women, whereas I think a lot of men start businesses because it sounds as though they are going to make a lot of money.

For me, if I find a client with a new business that has a great product or service, I want to work with them so they are able to grow their business and in turn become long term clients. It's not about charging high prices either. It's about helping other businesses grow. I think the other major component for women business owners is the personal satisfaction of liking your job and wanting to show up every day. I've been running this business for the last 2 years on a low income and haven't taken a paycheck, so it's definitely not about the money for me. It's drive and not being willing to give up or stop.

What is your personal definition of success, and have you achieved it?

I'm not quite sure. I definitely don't feel like I've achieved it. I'm sure there is a generic answer of wanting to be financially independent, loving my work, and being able to have the time and resources to take a vacation, and be proud of what it is that I'm accomplishing. I don't think it is about awards, either. They can have a lot of favoritism attached to them. How my business is successful means that it is actually running in the black and our clients would be successful because of the work that we are doing. Also, success looks like the people working here love their work; I want the entire team to have satisfaction and growth in their work. I am definitely too much my job right now, so I don't spend enough effort to make that balance that would be a part of success for me.

What didn't I ask you about you and your business that you wanted me to?

Personally, my business is about collaboration and believing in what I'm doing. Yes, it would be nice to be totally famous and have tons of clients, but I'm not there yet. I think the other thing too that I am really grateful for is that I have the opportunity to share my knowledge. Teaching is a really great way to learn how to delegate and teach your staff. I did teach at the Academy of Arts for a while, and it helps with public speaking, delegation, critiquing, and communicating with others and customers. Giving back and sharing your knowledge are super important!

Robbin Jorgensen

The Bold Impact Group

Robbin Jorgensen, *founder and CEO of The Bold Impact Group, is a successful businesswoman with 15 years of experience in sales and marketing, training and business development. Robbin began her sales career working with the American Heart Association as Director of Corporate Relations. At the AHA, Robbin recruited and trained hundreds of volunteers and was responsible for raising several million dollars through corporate sponsorships and fundraising activities. In addition, she developed and presented numerous training programs at local, statewide and national conferences including: Building Corporate Relationships, Creating Customer Loyalty, Customer Retention, and Developing Recognition and Cultivation Programs. Robbin was awarded the Heart Association's New York State Business Development Award for her accomplishments. Robbin continued her sales career in newspaper advertising with the Hearst Corporation where she was responsible for running a multi-million dollar classified vertical, held various sales and management roles and won numerous sales* *awards for her accomplishments. As interactive sales director for Hearst Media Services, she was responsible for developing sales teams in multiple markets and increasing the digital sales of the group to several million dollars within the first year with a focus on social media advertising solutions. Robbin has a passion for sales and a strong desire to help sales teams achieve success. She accomplishes this by impacting sales teams and organizations around the country with empowering, inspiring and impactful programs.*

The Bold Impact Group *is a sales training and coaching company that challenges sales teams to approach things differently. We've all heard the saying—"If you keep doing what you've always done, you'll always get what you've always gotten." Well? It's time to put some BOLD IMPACT into sales behavior and change that! They work through those habits that hold salespeople back, help them break through those walls and become the salespeople that make an IMPACT not only for their customers and themselves, but the bottom line. They do more than just traditional training. They incorporate experiential learning into all of their programs. This type of learning allows an individual to see for themselves what is working and what isn't. When people become aware of their patterns of behavior they can choose to keep them or change them. In addition, they work with the sales leaders through coaching programs that address the issues that they face in managing the sales team. It is the powerful combination of sales training and coaching that creates exponential change and results. Contact them today to put some BOLD IMPACT into your sales! Their website is: www.theboldimpactgroup.com.*

Can you describe your business in one sentence?

The Bold Impact Group inspires sales organizations through training and coaching programs and empowers them to take action that creates lasting results.

What advantages do you think you have as a single/divorced solo business owner that married people don't have?

By Erin Albert

I think as a single/divorced woman entrepreneur, I am able to function at a higher level (get more done) because I am only accountable to myself. My time is my own and I get to choose how to spend it. Also, there is an empowerment that comes with knowing that I am accomplishing my dreams and my goals on my own terms.

What about disadvantages?
As a single business owner, you are responsible, good or bad, for your decisions. It can be a disadvantage to not have a partner to bounce ideas off of or to have a team of resources to rely on.

Do you think business ownership has led you to remain single?
No. I don't think being a business owner has swayed me one way or the other. Although I am technically single, I have an incredible man in my life who has encouraged my dreams and supported me every step of the way in starting my business. However, I do think that having someone you trust offer feedback and suggestions on your ideas can be very helpful and perhaps offer other perspectives.

What advice would you give another single woman who is thinking about starting a business?
I would tell her that one of the most important things you have to do is to believe in yourself. Believe in your own potential and your own greatness—that you have the power to create any life you can imagine. Know that you CAN do it. Visualize yourself succeeding. Create a vision statement that has you looking back at your business from 10 years in the future. What have you accomplished? What dreams have you realized? How have you impacted your community, and your world? This is an exercise that I learned through participating in the Big Fish Nation* program and it was instrumental in taking my company to the next level. You actually begin to see those dreams unfold and begin to take shape—very powerful.

I would also encourage her to work with a coach along the journey. Having a mentor to challenge you, encourage you, and hold you accountable to your vision is invaluable. Every professional athlete has a coach that functions in the same capacity. Think of where your favorite athlete would be without her or his coach. You will achieve so much more and in much less time with that partner at your side. Living your true purpose is truly incredible. Go for it!

* *[You can learn more about coaching from Big Fish Nation at: www.bigfishnation.com.]*

Do you think there are advantages/disadvantages to being a single business owner? Do you think it is harder, or easier?

One of the advantages of being a single business owner is that you have the authority to make all of the decisions regarding your business. You don't have to go through a chain of command because you are that chain of command. Your ideas and your vision can come to fruition based on your own volition.

One of the disadvantages to being a single business owner is that you don't have the corporate resources available to you that you may have had in your prior job. Those resources are easily taken for granted until they are not there to utilize when you wish. Another disadvantage is that there are only so many hours in a day. As a single business owner, there are many times you wish you could clone yourself to get everything done.

How do you manage around this problem?

To maximize my time, every morning I set my daily intentions. I look at my "to do" list and focus on three things that I need to get done that day and do my best to accomplish those tasks before moving on to other things. Getting those items crossed off gives me a sense of accomplishment and re-energizes me to work through the rest of the list. I also try my best to delegate items to my virtual assistant.

What about being a single WOMAN business owner?
Do you think it is easier, the same, or harder than being a single man starting a business?

By Erin Albert

Being a woman business owner is extremely powerful. I think there are just as many opportunities afforded to women as men in business ownership. Women also have incredible resources available to them that provide wonderful services and programs to assist them with their business such as NAWBO, The National Association of Women Business Owners, and Big Fish Nation, mentioned previously and below.

What was the best training you received to prepare you as a business owner?

Some of the best training I received was participating in a women's entrepreneurial coaching and training program called Big Fish Nation. Lorin Beller-Blake, founder and CEO of Big Fish Nation, has been an entrepreneur many times over and developed this program specifically for women business owners. The year-long course walks you through every aspect of owning a business including goal setting, SWOT (strengths, weaknesses, opportunities and threats) analysis, determining your values and your long term vision, sales and marketing.

It also integrates a spiritual approach to business development and affords you the privilege of working with amazing women who become your friends, your support system, and your Big Fish Nation family. Most importantly, the program challenges your thinking, empowers you to reach past what you think is possible and holds you accountable to your vision by helping you take decisive, bold action that moves you in the direction of your goals and dreams.

I also was fortunate to be able to participate in an Empowerment Mentoring program with Les Brown, one of the nation's premier motivational speakers, and Paul Martinelli, an amazing coach and master of personal development. This program is designed to take you out of your comfort zone and encourages you to reach beyond what you think is possible for yourself. This was also a year-long program that included bi-weekly coaching calls, training modules and an in-person think tank session with Les and Paul. Both of these programs truly changed my life, and I am eternally grateful.

Did you, or are you running your business as a part-time or full-time venture? Why?

The Bold Impact Group is a full-time venture. I love what I do. I am passionate about impacting sales teams and giving them the tools they need to accomplish bold results, so it is natural for me to want to engage in my business 24/7.

How important were mentors in your entrepreneurial career?

Vital. Mentors provide you with guidance, support, and encouragement. They hold you accountable to achieving your vision. Mentors provide that belief in your vision when you may not have that belief yourself. You borrow on their belief in you until you have the confidence and belief in yourself.

Did you start your business with your own capital?

I started The Bold Impact Group with my own capital. It was important to me to begin this venture and this next phase of my life without acquiring any debt to do it.

How important are your social and personal networks to the success of your business?

Both of these aspects have been an important component to my success. With my type of company, networking, promoting, and maintaining a consistent public presence for your brand is essential. Becoming involved in chambers, leading groups and utilizing social networking to get your company programs in front of as many people as possible are keys to being successful. I also have an incredible personal network that includes my significant other, a wonderful family and great friends who all support me and encourage me every step of the way.

Why do you think more single/divorced and widowed women start more businesses than men in their respective categories, and does your theory match your own rationale for starting a business?

I think it is a way for women to break through that glass ceiling and run their careers on their own terms. It affords women the opportunity to call their own shots, set their own level of expectations of themselves, and not have to conform to another's way of thinking or corporate structure.

During my career in corporate America, I was given wonderful opportunities and moved up the corporate ladder rather quickly. However, I really felt a desire to break out on my own and start The Bold Impact Group. It was time for me to go for my dream of owning my own company and affecting change in sales organizations with my own programs and messages.

A lot of women struggle with the 'sign' for starting their own businesses. What made it time for you to break out on your own? Was there a watershed moment for you, or just a growing gut feeling over time?

I have always been drawn to reading motivational and self help books. While away on vacation in April, 2010, I brought along some financial books that included: *The Millionaire Next Door, Smart Women Finish Rich* and *The Millionaire Mind.* One of the recurring themes throughout all of the books was the connection between financial independence and entrepreneurship. That began to plant the seed for me. Over Memorial Day weekend, I was finishing one of the books from vacation and truly had an "A-ha!" moment. I started to feel empowered and knew that starting this business was what I was meant to do. I realized that I could use my experience and my skill sets to impact sales organizations around the country and truly create the life I've always wanted, not only financially, but in terms of work/life balance. I just knew the timing was right and I haven't looked back since.

What is your personal definition of success, and have you achieved it?

What a great question! My personal definition of success is being able to live your true life's purpose. Being confident in who you are, having the belief in yourself that you can achieve ANYTHING you want in life and impacting others' lives in a positive way. I always want to stay in growth mode both personally and professionally and continue to improve upon my programs and my message, so I would say that I always want to be striving to achieve more.

Patti
Justice

Blooming Pregnancy Spa & Imaging Center

Patti Justice *was born and raised in Austin, TX, and she is convinced it is the best city on Earth. She was engaged in 1993 and left Austin to pursue her "American Dream," which used to consist of education, career, marriage and children. It did not work out as planned. She ended that journey with a B.A. in Visual Art, 6 years of professional experience as a graphic artist, an ex-husband she still calls a friend, and two beautiful stepdaughters, (one of which now has two of her own children!) and a vision for what her new "American Dream" would look like. It consists of a woman owning her destiny, making her own rules about happiness, being passionate, authentic, and then maybe marriage and children.*

Blooming Pregnancy Spa & Imaging Center was finally "born" in August, 2010. It is the ONLY full service spa in Austin that caters to expecting women. Every treatment they offer is designed with the expecting women's needs in mind, including the use of all organic and non-toxic products. They are serving the community of motherhood in a very special and much deserved way. Find it online at: www.bloomingpregnancyspa.com.

Single. Women. Entrepreneurs.

Can you describe your business in one sentence?

Blooming Pregnancy Spa & Imaging Center celebrates the body, mind and spirit of motherhood before, during and after pregnancy.

What is your business concept and was it derived from personal experience?

The concept behind Blooming was about creating a service for local mothers, which would create an opportunity to reach out on a larger scale. I believe that empowered mothers raise empowered children, which will ultimately lead to a better world. One of my goals is for Blooming to adopt a different charity each quarter throughout the year that supports mothers and children in various parts of the world. This is my personal way of enabling that process of empowerment!

What advantages do you think you have as a single/divorced solo business owner that married people don't have?

As a divorced woman business owner, I am forced to own each and every decision I make, which is a huge advantage simply for the learning aspect. I don't feel the "need" to get approval for any of my business decisions from a spouse. I think some married women may feel that need, which essentially holds them back.

What about disadvantages?

One disadvantage that I experienced was not having a second income to help curve the fear when things got tight. I was also scrutinized by banks a lot harder because I did not have a spouse … it seemed I needed three times the collateral of what I would have needed if I had a spouse's income to serve as a security net.

Do you think business ownership has led you to remain single?

Yes and no! Being a business owner is brand new and has actually led me to meet many new and interesting people that I never would have met otherwise. However, the years leading up to the opening of my business were so consumed by that responsibility that my dating life definitely suffered.

They say entrepreneurs attract other entrepreneurs—did you?

I am still single! But I am dating someone right now who is very business-minded. He shares my passion for creating new things, so maybe there is truth to entrepreneurs attracting the same … I hope so!

What advice would you give another single woman who is thinking about starting a business?

Be ready to work! Be clear, be strong, and LEARN from every disappointing experience rather that feel like it was a setback. Have a vision for what you want, and own it! Don't rely too much on the advice of others, because only you know what your vision looks and feels like.

Do you think there are advantages/disadvantages to being a single business owner? Do you think it is harder, or easier?

I would love to have a spouse to help with the element of life balance. I can handle running the business … but if I had help with laundry, groceries, car maintenance, and just the general day to day responsibilities of being a contributing member of society, then yes, it would be easier if I had a husband! However, since I am single, I have the luxury of creating my own schedule and do not have the competing priorities a marriage would bring.

What about being a single WOMAN business owner?
Do you think it is easier, the same, or harder than being a single man starting a business?

In the case of being a single business owner, I think being a woman is definitely an advantage. Women are wired to be nurturing AND multi-taskers. So we can navigate through the responsibilities of running a business without neglecting other things. It's not easy, but doable. I'm not saying that men aren't capable of being nurturing multi-taskers, but women are better at it! Married men, however, have it the easiest as business owners. They have a spouse who is most likely picking up the slack in other areas of life, like the day to day stuff I mentioned earlier, which affords them more focused time for their business.

What was the best training you received to prepare you as a business owner?

It was a combination of things. I went through tremendous personal growth with Big Fish Nation, a year long committed program for woman business owners. At the time, I was just a business owner wannabe. I realized that having faith in the business vision was important, but having faith in myself was the key! I combined that with the knowledge of how I did and did not want to run a business compiled from the years of experience working for others, and liking or not liking the methods they used!

Did you, or are you running your business as a part-time or full-time venture? Why?

This is totally full-time. For my business, it was all or nothing. I had reached the point in my life where I needed to go BIG or change direction all together. Now, one of my favorite mottos is, "Go big, or go home!"

Did you take on a partner in your business at any time?

I started out without a partner, and then brought one on board to help secure funding, and to provide experience in business management. Personal reasons caused her to back out. She eventually came back, and then backed out again ... I realized this was a red flag and that the vision I had was not the same as hers. My thoughts on "needing" a partner changed as I grew more confident in myself. Now, being the sole owner, I would not have it any other way. Partnerships are tough. I would advise any business owner to be very clear on any partner's ideas and long-term goals before letting them be a part of their dream.

By Erin Albert

If you had to start another business, what have you learned that you might do differently—either about yourself, or about how to run a business in general?

So many things! This has been the most educational thing I have ever done, and all the lessons were learned the hard way. What I would do differently is rely less on the opinions of others and trust my instincts, research answers for myself, and understand ALL the dynamics of a commercial lease ... (such as building inspections before you sign the dotted line, store front signage criteria, and a tenant improvement allowance ... just to name a few!)

How important were mentors in your entrepreneurial career?

HUGE! Finding the right mentors was essential in keeping me going. Listening to them and learning from their examples was very valuable, but relating to them on a personal level made me more confident. I learned that my insecurities were just as normal as many other very successful business owners.

Did you start your business with your own capital?

Ahhh, funding. This was the hardest piece for me. I was divorced, without a safety net or full-time income. I was depending on a dream and a prayer! I approached at least a dozen different funding sources including banks and non-profit lending agencies. They all said no. Each time I heard "No," it was followed with, "But you have an excellent business plan and idea!" That was very frustrating, but I realized that getting the right investor was not so much about them believing in my business; they had to believe in me. That led me to approach my immediate family members, who had witnessed my efforts and understood my level of dedication. They decided to jump in and put all their faith in ME. We got creative with mortgages and credit cards and now the business is open ... and doing well!

How important are your social and personal networks to the success of your business?

Single. Women. Entrepreneurs.

They are essential! Networking leads to one opportunity after another. I have many supporters simply by networking with the right people. My business has an affiliated OB/GYN (which is crucial to gaining credibility with the medical community) that was introduced to me through a mutual friend. Had I not been constantly talking about my business ideas and needs, this introduction would never have happened.

Why do you think more single/divorced and widowed women start more businesses than men in their respective categories, and does your theory match your own rationale for starting a business?

For me, and probably many other women, I did not want to ever (again) feel dependant on a man, which is exactly what I felt when I first divorced. Of course, I did not want to admit that to anyone, or even myself. So, I had to reinvent myself in a big way. As a woman, I wanted to be whole and strong, and completely self sufficient in every way ... including financially!

What is your personal definition of success, and have you achieved it?

Let me paraphrase the last sentence above ... my definition of success is to be whole, and strong, and completely self sufficient in every way! This includes the ability to be happy and balanced with or without a husband. Yes, I have achieved that.

What other single women business owners do you admire, and why?

Oprah! She's a category all unto her own. I have a friend from high school who launched her own business after a divorce and catapulted herself into the boys' arena of high tech. Her company was last valued at 3 million! The key ingredient that I admire about her, and Oprah, and other successful women is their refusal to be defined by a relationship. These women define themselves! This ties in to the way I view personal success.

Kristin Kuhlke

Cupcake

Kristin Kuhlke *is 38 years young and lives in Charleston, South Carolina. She grew up mostly in Pennsylvania and went to college at Clemson University in South Carolina where she earned a bachelor's degree in financial management. Kristin is a major foodie and loves to cook and eat out. Meals are the best part of her day. She is also a runner and loves to spend time boating. Kristin loves living in Charleston and spending time with her boyfriend, Darryl, and their three dogs—Max, Tobi and Wriggly.*

Cupcake, founded by Kristin Kuhlke, opened its doors in March 2006. They serve yummy cupcake concoctions from their stores in downtown Charleston, Mt. Pleasant, and Columbia, South Carolina ... and a new fourth location coming soon! Cupcake also cleverly donates yesterday's cupcakes to not for profit and charity causes. You can find them on the web at: www.freshcupcakes.com, on Facebook (Cupcake), and Twitter (@freshcupcakes).

Single. Women. Entrepreneurs.

Ok, most important question first: can you overnight your cupcakes?

We can, but we try not to. Our cupcakes are baked fresh every day with only fresh ingredients—no preservatives. So to ship, we usually need to freeze them. Also, we cannot control temperatures during shipping and our cupcakes come with a giant swirl of icing on them—real icing, made with butter—so they don't fare too well in the heat or if they get tossed around. We were featured on Martha Stewart radio a while back and had to ship them up to NYC for the interview. They ate the cupcakes on air and said they were delicious—but I can only imagine how they might have looked!

What advantages do you think you have as a single woman business owner that married women might not have?

I can focus on the business without other distractions. I've had to make so many decisions and take so many risks that I might not have taken had there been another person involved in my decision making process. I could decide which direction to go using my own instinct and not relying on anyone else. It was liberating.

Also, my job can be very cyclical. Sometimes I have so much on my plate that I'm working all the time. Other times I have lots of free time. So when I need to devote my full attention to my business, I don't have to worry about taking time away from a husband or children. I can just concentrate on the task at hand.

Right now, when my plate gets too full, I have to hire people to take over some of these responsibilities. Before I open a store, I set myself up so I can completely focus on the new store. I'm getting ready to launch a fourth location with a slightly different concept than my other stores (more of a full dessert and coffee bar). So, I need to have everything running smoothly with the other three stores so that I can devote the majority of my time to the new location. My plan for my business has always been to grow it to multiple locations. So I go in, start a new store, upfit, hire, train, and then teach others how to run it. Then I slowly back myself out of it and start over again. It is kind of like running or starting a new business within a business. I have the vision for how I want a particular store to operate, and then I have a great staff that can carry out the plan.

My best friend started in my downtown store, then became general manager of my second store, then had a baby and became my office assistant in charge of ordering, donations and emails. Now she is director of operations and oversees all of the staff. She's a key employee of the business. She works part-time because she's also a mom. She commands the staff and still does a lot of work from home. I have a lot of women working in my company who now have babies, so there's a lot of opportunity to be creative in order to retain these great women in my business.

How do you do that, because a lot of women who want to start families struggle with balancing work and starting a family ...?

We try to hire people who we want to stick around. I still think of myself as this tiny little company, but we're at almost 50 employees now. When we find people who care about the company and what we're doing, I want them to stay in whatever capacity they can. I've actually had five women who, shortly after being hired at Cupcake, got pregnant and had babies. Three are still with me, one moved away, and the last is trying to come back if we can find something to fit her needs. I feel that family comes first; so, when you need to take care of your family, that takes priority. But if we can work them back into the system somehow, then it only helps the company, because we have a stronger team that cares about where they work and what they do. It has worked out well, because we're kind of a big family.

What disadvantages do you perceive being a single woman business owner?

Not having as much financial support. That's a positive and a negative. If I had a second income, I might take more risk, or I might not. Maybe I make better and wiser decisions because I know there's no one else paying the bills. Any and every business owner is a risk taker. But, maybe if you're not depending on that income as much for your livelihood, you will be wiser about decisions. I feel if I had been married through all of this, I never would have taken this business as far as I have taken it. My focus would be different.

I'm probably the oldest of all of my girlfriends, and I'm the only business owner. The focus shifts when you're married. I am getting married in one week myself. I don't know if my priorities are going to shift or not, but I still have the same goals and dreams. I struggle with the idea of having a family and wonder—how am I going to do it all? If I had already been in that place mentally, I wouldn't have been opening all these stores. Maybe I'd only have one store and I'd be an owner/operator instead of having managers.

Congratulations on getting married! They say entrepreneurs attract other entrepreneurs—did you?

Yes, he is an entrepreneur. He owns his own architectural firm. I found that to be an attractive quality in him, and we have VERY different businesses, but we can bounce ideas off of each other. I'm way more of a risk taker than he is; he's much more conservative. I actually met him while I was setting cupcakes up for a wedding of one of his friends.

When I left the corporate world I was actually dating someone else. He couldn't believe I was going to start my own business with the little money that I had. He told me I needed to have two million dollars in the bank to start a business. I thought, if I had two million dollars in the bank, I wouldn't NEED to start my own business. It always makes me chuckle to think about him.

What advice would you give another single woman who is thinking about starting a business?

I get this all the time. My best advice is to do your homework. Before I started my business, I read books and talked to people; I was a sponge. You have to have a good balance of knowledge and facts along with a gut feeling and a desire. The statistics on the number of businesses failing in the first few years are horribly sobering. You may challenge yourself thinking you must be crazy to start this venture, but if you have a strong desire to do it and believe in what you're doing, then you work around the crazy. You have to really know that you've found the right business for who you are.

For a long time, I knew I wanted my own business, but I wasn't sure what business would exactly be right for me. I moved to New York City, which provided me with tons of ideas, and came back to South Carolina to try the cupcake thing. It was a good fit for me because cooking and baking are passions of mine. Also, I had a background in business and finance. I wasn't just a baker trying to open a business; I was a businessperson who loved to bake. Although I hadn't worked in a bakery, I had worked in many food and beverage establishments, had done bookkeeping jobs, sales jobs, worked for small businesses, etc. All of these positions helped teach me lessons along the way. I was finally ready to wear all of the hats of owning my own business. I think sometimes that's where people go wrong. You need to know your strengths and weaknesses. With me, I had an accounting background, so I could do my own books for a couple of years. By the time it was too much for me and I needed to hire someone, I had the money to do so. And another important piece of advice—pay your bills. After starting my first store and borrowing a small amount of money, I paid the loan off and have not borrowed anything since then. I slowly upgraded my equipment as my business grew, instead of buying the best and newest from the start and getting into huge amounts of debt. I wouldn't have survived the slow times if I had large loan payments to make each month.

Also, don't be afraid to make mistakes. I know I don't have all the answers. It's a whole learning experience every single day as an entrepreneur. It's very rewarding when you think back to where you've come from and how much you've learned as a business owner over time ... it's exciting to think you'll continue that as you grow.

Single. Women. Entrepreneurs.

What about being a single WOMAN business owner? Did you ever feel discounted as a woman business owner?

No, I'm not really looking for anyone's recognition. I think when I started all of this there were lots of people who didn't take me seriously. But I don't mind. I get to have the last laugh.

What was the best training you received to prepare you as a business owner?

I wanted to own my own business for a long time, but I would say my training was gradual. I believe all of the jobs I had previous to starting my business aided my success. My year spent living in NYC was largely used for gathering ideas. I had a bunch of sales jobs prior to starting my business, and I met so many people through those jobs. I picked people's brains and learned from them. I got advice. The best piece of advice I ever received was from a customer of mine when I worked in the cell phone industry. He owned his own business and told me—do it on your own, don't have a partner. At the time I was hoping to partner with my best friend and I'm SO GLAD he gave me the gift of that advice. I am so strong-minded and know what I want to do, so to have a partner would be extremely difficult for me. I really only wanted a partner because I was afraid of failure and thought it wouldn't hurt so much if I had someone else going through it with me. He had a partner originally and bought him out, so he lived that experience. By being solo, you don't have to ask permission for everything related to the business.

There's never going to be the perfect moment to start a business, and the timing will never be exactly perfect. But, there are moments where you know you're fully committed. I had two moments: 1. When I came up with the idea and went to dinner with my best friend and told her about it. 2. When I found the space for my first store and signed the lease. It was like instant anxiety. I couldn't believe I was doing it!

By Erin Albert

Did you ever obtain outside financing or a loan?

I got an equity line of credit from my house. Fortunately, the space I found for my first store had been a café. I had a friend who was a general contractor who obtained my permits, and my dad helped me reconstruct the store. I found another friend who built all my cabinets. I started off with the bare minimum and slowly bought higher-grade equipment when I could afford it. I didn't do any advertising initially either, and literally walked up and down the streets handing out cupcakes and telling people to come and check us out. I slowly grew the business. Now, it is different, because I buy the equipment I need from the beginning and do tons of advertising. In retrospect, I don't think I would have been able to get a loan even if I wanted one, because I was in the riskiest category business type (a restaurant) and South Carolina back then didn't understand a cupcake business.

Did you, or are you running your business as a part-time or full-time venture?

I went full-time. I signed the first lease in November of 2005 and quit my job in December 2005. I started the New Year with NO INCOME. I was scared to death. I opened the doors of my first location March 17, 2006 and I was just praying I could pay myself and my bills! I don't necessarily recommend this way of doing things—it's risky.

How did you deal with the fear?

In looking back, I have to say that the business wasn't the first time I took a risk. When I turned 30, I bought my first house. Then a year later, I bought a second house and rented the first. I had gutted and remodeled the first house with the help of my dad and best friend. Fortunately, I had two roommates to help pay the rent. When I bought the second house, I had a stomachache for a month straight: from the time I signed the papers at closing to the time I leased the first house. I questioned myself: who do I think I am buying two houses? I sold cell phones and made

$40,000 a year! Houses were still reasonably priced back then and banks were still loaning money. So, I think I had done some things along the way to work through the excitement and the fear of opening a business.

Also, I worked in food and beverage and various jobs before, and I wasn't above going back. I knew I could always go get a job to make money to pay my bills. When I got out of college and was in my twenties, I was stupid with money and had a lot of credit card bills, but I paid them off, and then started buying houses. I also realized I didn't want to borrow a ton of money to start the business. I paid for my second and third stores with profits from the previous stores; I never took loans for growing the business. Honestly, I don't know if I would have made it through this economic downturn if I had taken out loans for the business.

I still have fear, because I always worry that I'm going to open a new store and it will fail. The new store is my new stomachache, but it is exciting and it drives me to work harder to succeed. I get to put my own creative touch on things and I have the greatest job in the world.

Were your parents entrepreneurs?

No. My dad recently passed away, but he was so proud of me through all this. It tickled him to hear about what I was up to with the business. My mom was a music teacher and she doesn't have this entrepreneurial bone at all … it just blows her mind. My dad thought it was great, but it scares her to death. My dad was a salesman and a navy pilot—he could build anything, do anything—he was Superman! I have that in me because we remodeled these homes together and he also helped me start the first store. Business and financial aspects weren't his forte, but the creativity was in his blood.

I love your idea about donating yesterday's cupcakes to charities. How did you come up with that idea?

This is really important to me, because I feel very blessed by God to be where I am. With this opportunity of business ownership and success, I feel very responsible for giving back to my community and teaching my staff the importance of that. Technically, I never had a trade. I wasn't trained to be a doctor or an architect. However, I had different jobs, and they each somehow came together and led me to do what I'm doing now. Without the community supporting me, I wouldn't be here. I want to build a business, but I REALLY want to make a difference. I believe that is why I have been given a voice. I want my staff to understand that too.

Because we bake our cupcakes fresh every day, we had to decide, where do all the leftovers go? You can touch a lot of lives with a little treat. In the cell phone business, I figured out that about eighty percent of the people were coming in to complain. So, everyday, I felt like I got beat up. I decided that I wanted to do something that makes people happy! So when I opened Cupcake, the smell and the experience just gets people excited and happy when they come and visit us! It is so rewarding for me.

Now, when we can take the leftovers somewhere, like Ronald McDonald House or another charity, it makes their day. We now have one of our employees whose sole job is working out all the logistics of the donations for each store each day. Also, we are trying to piggyback onto local non profit efforts. We are giving away our cupcakes and our time. I know that getting involved helps the community, but really, at the end of the day, getting involved gives me more than what I give in return. This year, we got involved in the Susan G. Komen Race for the Cure. Cupcake was a gold sponsor, and we were involved in several ways. We sold paper cherries in the store for $1 each. I originally printed 100 paper cherries for each of the three stores we had open, and they all sold out within two days, so we had to print more. We ended up selling over 3,000. We also had a special commemorative cupcake that we sold every day in October. For each cupcake we sold, $1 went to Susan G. Komen Foundation. We sold over $4,000 of those cupcakes. We donated mini cupcakes to various events, and had a team in the race too. It was fun for the staff to be involved.

We are also getting involved in kids' programs at schools about how to grow food and be conscious of what they eat. We believe in fresh ingredients and we are just at the very beginning stages of this. We are partnering with Share our Strength, the Great American Bake Sale, and Family Circle—they help us figure out how to get more involved locally.

I'm so impressed with TOMS shoes and their business model—the idea of giving something away when something sells. So, for every party we do for little girls, or a baking party for kids where they learn and decorate their own cupcakes, we are trying to go to an underprivileged area of the city and also throw a party. Baking was such a family thing for me. There is a nostalgic feeling of family and togetherness that kids should be part of in order to see what a true joy baking can be. That's what we are on the path to do; try to get super involved in the community. When people come in, we want them to know we are not just out here to chase the almighty dollar.

What is your personal definition of success, and have you achieved it?

I believe I have, just because I'm happy, I love my job, and my business. I never put a dollar sign on this business from the very start. I never said, if I make $XXX, then I will have succeeded; so I'm always surprised by what we do. I think that is one of the reasons we've stuck around and have grown despite this economy. We're not always selling for the top dollars. We really work to keep the staff happy, which in turn helps us be a more effective team, which helps to make a great and consistent product to serve to our community. If it all ended tomorrow, I would feel like I have done everything I wanted to do and more. I'm so thankful for the opportunity to come as far as we have. What a great ride it's been!

Any other points not covered?

I only have one point about women not being taken seriously, which we discussed a little before. Women owned businesses are growing quickly, and I think this makes sense. If women can manage

By Erin Albert

a household with kids, a husband, family, etc., beautifully, why can't we run a business beautifully too? We are used to wearing a lot of hats. We can be soft and hard when we need to be. Knowing when to be sweet and when to bark is helpful. Being a business owner, you'll find yourself being emotional about it at times, and that's not a terrible thing. It matters to you. I think being a woman gives you an advantage as a business owner. Embrace it.

Darla
LeDoux

Doux Coaching

Darla **LeDoux** is a Certified Professional Coach, "recovering engineer," owner of **Doux Coaching**, and creator of **Destination: Sweet Spot**. She is fueled by a passion for people being who they truly are, exactly as they are, in business and in life, living in their sweet spot. In the sweet spot one uses their unique combination of gifts, talents, and passions having maximum impact, with ease.

After spending 15 years in "successful" careers working for others—product development engineering, marketing, and education—the things she thought she "should" do to be successful, Darla found the courage to step into her sweet spot and follow the desires of her heart. She absolutely loves helping others do the same, without spending 10+ years in the self-help aisle.

Darla works with people in all stages of transition and reinvention, who have tried doing life and business the "right" way, and are now ready to listen to that deep inner knowledge and discover what is truth for them. She coaches them to begin being who they need to be

131

to have the life they desire now, not someday. Darla can be reached via her website at www.DouxCoaching.com.

Can you describe your business in one sentence?

I help people to get clarity about, and confidence in, their own natural brilliance, and what they want their life to look like, so they design their work and life to work for them.

What type(s) of clients do you coach?

I have two major types of clients. Most of them are new business owners who want to design their business in a way that works for them—either something they're doing isn't working, or they are giving themselves away or working too hard. The other type of clients I coach are high achievers in their corporate career, but are unfulfilled. Many of them also have entrepreneurial dreams that are deeply hidden. That's where I came from. I have a heart for people who don't know what they want to be when they grow up—I didn't for years.

Why did you start your business?

Two reasons, really. I knew that this—coaching—was my calling. It is the way for me to make the difference I am here to make, and it uses my natural talents. I love to support people in making their work and lives better; specifically, to feel as if they can be free to be themselves in all areas of their lives, knowing their talents are valuable, and that it is OK if there are things they are just not good at, or don't like (for example, I am good at math, but don't love to do it). That acceptance is the key to being happy and expressed in one's work, and working with ease. I love helping people get there.

My own personal clarity about starting my business came when my stepdad was diagnosed with cancer and passed away three months after diagnosis. I didn't have the chance to spend as much time with him as I wanted, because I was working in a career where I had to be in the office. I only had so many vacation days. I didn't spend as much time with my stepdad as I would have liked. Now, with my coaching, I can work from anywhere. That is personally important to me.

What are the advantages to being a single business owner? What about disadvantages?

I think there are many. When you're a single business owner, you're the only person you can rely on for your income. That can be scary. The flip side occurs when I coach married entrepreneurs and one of their extra hurdles is having a conversation with their spouse about starting a business, or getting buy-in to invest in their business. Getting the spouse on board for a married entrepreneur can be a challenge, especially because it is usually the entrepreneur who is changing gears. Their spouses aren't bad people, and the check-in can be a benefit, but it is often an extra step for married people to have that conversation with their spouse about trying something new. When you're single, that is one less step to take. You, alone, can choose your level of risk.

One disadvantage is financial; you're on your own as a single person. I think that's the main one. I also see some couples in business together who support each other well emotionally and that's a beautiful thing. As a single business owner, you don't necessarily have that. You can, however, find that support in other ways.

What is the difference between entrepreneurial thinking in starting one's own business and intrapreneurial thinking in corporate America that you see in your clients?

I do a lot of my work with people around tapping into their intuition, which corporate people in our culture can be out of touch with. One of the things that is beautiful about being an entrepreneur is that you get to use your intuition. In a corporation, there might be seven levels of decision-making above an individual, and by the time a great idea moves up those seven levels, the decisions only become rational, analytical, and data-driven. The brilliance of an idea doesn't always make rational sense. Most big innovations came from someone's crazy idea. When you're in a corporate environment, those ideas don't usually see the light of day.

Do you think business ownership has led you to remain single?

No, running my business is just my favorite thing to do right now, because my business is a creation of my passions and is heartfelt for me. In terms of spending my time, I'd rather be working in my business and I'd rather not be doing anything else ... including dating. I have been married, which didn't last for reasons unrelated to my career, and I am sure I will marry again. I love being in a relationship. We can only have so many priorities in life, and I would say I am taking advantage of being single to grow my business and create a structure that allows me time for a full life, including a partner. It won't take long!

They say entrepreneurs attract other entrepreneurs in life—do you think so?

That's an interesting question. Because my background is corporate, a lot of my friends are still in the corporate world. A lot of the entrepreneurs I meet become clients. I'm thinking now about making more entrepreneur friends. I made friends with a lot of entrepreneurs all over the country while taking training. I've recently created the intention of having more entrepreneurial friends. I could see that entrepreneurs attract other entrepreneurs— it would be convenient.

How do you perceive entrepreneurs as thinkers—how do they think differently from others?

Entrepreneurs look at everything as an opportunity. I see that we tend to look for what is possible in a situation, and also to approach most situations from a standpoint of feeling empowered—as if our opinions and needs matter. An employee mindset is often one of looking for evidence of the limits, and, often subconsciously, assuming that someone else is going to tell them what is important. People can have an entrepreneurial mindset and still work within a company. People who start businesses but don't learn to think like an entrepreneur will struggle.

To connect this thinking back to your questions about being single or in a relationship, and whether we tend to attract other entrepreneurs, here is an example. As an entrepreneur, I have ideas about how I want my want my life to look like and I fully believe I will have it. If I'm dating someone who has a job, and a job-mindset, that idea might not become reality, because that person will have to worry about where their job or career is located, and might see obstacles rather than opportunity. The significant other who thinks entrepreneurially might build on my vision, and say, "Let's pull out a map and pick a place where BOTH of us can be happy." Entrepreneurs like to build on ideas and make them happen.

What advice would you give another single woman who is thinking about starting a business?

Hire a coach, of course. I think the first thing is to set the intention that you would like to attract a good coach. Whenever a client gets clear on what they need next, that person will appear. You might have met that person anyway, but we draw people into our lives, and notice them, based upon our energy and our intentions.

As soon as you decide what it is you want in a coach (someone to hold you accountable, someone to help you think bigger, someone to help you value your gifts, etc.) you'll notice people around you who are matches … and those who are not. The individual needs to know what they're looking for in a coach. If someone is reading this interview and knows they need someone like me, they can call me, just get into action. Whether me or someone else, a coach makes a big difference. I even have my own coach.

In choosing a coach, look for someone who is going to dig into you and what's important to you rather than handing you a formula. Following someone else's formula is NOT the path to fulfillment. A good coach will draw your brilliance out of you rather than telling you how to be like them. Advice is helpful, but only once you "know thyself."

I think the other thing to note, at least for me—it was important to hire someone who was ahead of me in business. Money is energy, and investing money in myself and my business (when it comes from an authentic place of moving toward what I love, rather than from fear of missing something) has always paid off. When you are clear on your intention, your money will come back to you and your business.

I can only speak from my path and the friends and clients I tend to attract—people who really want to make a difference—in their families and in the world. When your heart is in the business and you design your business around the difference you want to make, and you get the support you need, it really can't fail.

Businesses fail when they try to pursue something and chase a profit before they figure out what really is important to them. If you're running a business for the wrong reasons, it will drain you. You'll get tired and you'll quit. I was reading something recently, which said your purpose in your business has to be greater than yourself. If so, you're willing to get up every day and take the steps you need to take because you know in your heart that it is making a difference, and this big picture will draw your forward.

What was the best training you received to prepare you as a business owner?

I have to start by saying that I see everything that occurs in my life as training. We are constantly getting feedback from our world on what we are thinking and doing. Training is all around us. I have had a series of fantastic training and coursework opportunities. I did my coach training at iPEC Coaching. It is a phenomenal training program. I had coached before that, but this training took my coaching to another level. I also took a high-end mastermind program with an amazing coach. That opened my mind to see my business in a different way. But my passion comes from spending 10 years in a career I didn't love and reading every book in the self-help aisle trying to figure out what to do with my life. The self-help aisle was bad training. It is rare that a book can change our thinking dramatically (though I still love to read a ton), because we are always reading from our current level of awareness. What this did do for me was help me to understand how painful it is to not know your place or your purpose. When I was able to change my awareness (through coaching), what I wanted to do became clear and, honestly, easy. This pain is the fuel for my fire in my business today. I wouldn't replace that.

Did you, or are you, running your business as a part-time or full-time venture? Why?

Full-time. What happened that really had me launch is that my corporate business was bought, and I really didn't want to relocate. I was coaching on the side before the transition date, as I had made the decision to become an entrepreneur before that. I thought about getting a different job at that point and slowly building my business, then I realized that my severance package was a gift, and there was never a better time to be "all in." I did the math to see how long I could live without making any additional income. Then I gave myself the freedom to really focus on building my business rather than panicking about needing to make money ASAP or having to go back to a day job.

Honestly, I had no clue how much investment my business would take. And in reality, I had to start making money faster than I thought because I did invest in my business (training, coaching, website, and other business systems). But once I DECIDED to start my business and had money set aside and knew how long I had to live off of it, I committed myself to not focus on that. What we focus on, we put energy towards. I now coach others who are in this transition phase. You CANNOT think about when the money will run out, because then you subconsciously create ways for the money to run out. Plus, it is just not fun.

While it is very different for each individual how he or she does it, it is important to create a plan that will give you the freedom to build from a place of power, rather than living in fear. That is what is truly important. For some people, this requires a "transition job" to support their business, and for others they need to go "all in" to have the motivation needed to make it happen. When I work with people, we explore what level of risk is empowering to them, personally.

Did you take on a partner in your business at any time?

Not this time around. I mentioned I spent 10 years reading self-help books and working for companies, dreaming about a business. I had the entrepreneurial bug and explored partnerships during that time because I was afraid to do it alone. Today, I have referral partners who have their own businesses and I sometimes partner with them on projects. I am doing a fun workshop with a Yoga instructor next month. I love collaborating with people, but no partner. For my personal purpose, my business just needs to be my own.

Some people succeed in partnerships. I have a client who is in a 3-person partnership and it is working really well for them. Yet another client has a partner and each is in energetically different places right now, and the partnership isn't working very well. It is really hard for two people when they are not going in the same direction. As with any decision, if you choose to partner because you love the energy of it, great. If you are doing it out of fear of going it alone, I truly do not think it will work. This requires an honest look within for any entrepreneur.

If you had to start another business, what have you learned that you might do differently—either about yourself, or about how to run a business in general?

If I had to do it over again, I would do some things differently. I would worry less about the details and more about just talking with people and selling my services. I delayed a lot. I see this with my new clients as well. It is really easy to hide behind the rational, logical excuses. "When I have the perfect elevator pitch down, I'll be able to grow my business," or, "When my website is up and running I'll be able to take my business to the next level," are common. I don't spend a lot of time thinking about all the details in advance any more. Back when I started this business, I was worried about doing it right. Today, I would say FAIL FASTER. I probably heard that before, but it didn't register. The initial programs I created in my mind were a little off from what people wanted, and my original packages just didn't work. I had to instead get out and work with people and the programs developed organically.

The other thing is to hire a good bookkeeper early on. I think that most entrepreneurial people don't have brilliance in that arena. I have a client who is an accountant and she needed to hire a bookkeeper. It was a humbling experience for her, but doing your own books just stinks.

How important were mentors in your entrepreneurial career?

Mentors were and are extremely important. I didn't know a whole lot about entrepreneurship when I started. I had no family in business and no friends who were entrepreneurs. Like a lot of the corporate people I work with, I told myself initially I just wanted to make $3,000 per month and do work I loved. If I could just obtain that, I'd be happy. In other words, I had this idea that I was going to have sacrifice money to work for myself. That is not a bad place to start, because then the passion is present, which will take someone far.

Pretty early on in my business, I found a mentor who helped me see that actually working for yourself means you get to decide how much money you want to make. I am not the coach who pushes people to be millionaires—that decision has to come from them—however, I do now realize and I see in my own business, I can make whatever dollar amount I decide on and design for. Without that mentor, I am not sure that I would have seen that. And I might be struggling today.

I think it is so important to balance being confident in your talents and abilities while being aware that you don't know everything. For me, having a mentor ensures that I remain open to new ideas. It is also exciting for me to think that every couple of years I can change mentors and learn something new. I have the opportunity to do this now through my business, and this is exciting. I can pick a mentor I admire of my own choosing.

Single. Women. Entrepreneurs.

Did you start your business with your own capital?

Yes. As I said, it cost more than I expected; I had an inaccurate notion that it wouldn't cost anything to start this business. I hired a coach and took training. I designed for the business I knew I wanted to create, so I put some things in place early on that cost money (like a shopping cart online). I didn't want to do rework, and my severance package allowed me to do that. Funding and loans didn't even occur to me, because I didn't think it would cost much to start up. In retrospect, I might have applied for a loan before I quit my day job to start the business, but it really all worked out without a loan.

How important are your social and personal networks to the success of your business?

I think they are important, and will likely be even more important in the future. Initially, my social network contained mainly people from my corporate jobs. They were excited for me starting my own business and were great emotional support, but a lot of them can't fathom what my life is like now. Some of them have referred business to me. Mostly my clients have come in by "pounding the pavement" —networking, writing, speaking. Now that I am established, I will likely do more and more joint ventures with my network of other entrepreneurs who have complimentary businesses.

When should someone hire a coach, and what about the recession and its economic impact?

Now is always the perfect time. Not just for coaching, but for following your dreams. Ideas always come right on time, and in my opinion, we need to honor them. I think now is the best time to figure out "who you want to be when you grow up" and what success means to you.

I don't watch the news and don't listen to much on the radio, so I really don't acknowledge or follow the downturn in the economy. With the energy in our society, I have to be careful about what I choose to listen to. I started my business during the recession. I haven't struggled, because I have chosen not to struggle.

By Erin Albert

Why do you think more single/divorced and widowed women start more businesses than men in their respective categories?

I hate to categorize, but I think it is fascinating that women who are solo start more businesses than men. It may have to do with the personalities of the types of people who tend to start businesses, rather than their marital status.

I can speak for myself. Part of being an entrepreneur means that I'm not going to settle in my life; I have really high standards. I'll just go for it. I think that attitude might be different for women who are in a relationship with a significant other; it can take a lot of compromise to be in a relationship, or at least a traditional relationship.

Also, women are more integrated in terms of their lives. They think more holistically about their lives, whereas men can more easily compartmentalize. If I have someone in my life, for example, it would be important to me that they know about, understand, and support my business idea, because I can't easily separate. But a man might not care if his significant other knew about or understood his business because he can compartmentalize. I have also known a lot of men who had their wives work inside their businesses, but often in a support role.

Also, parenthood is a factor. Single mothers often realize that they don't want to waste their time with their children while working, and a flexible schedule is more important to them. Divorced or single men who are parents think more about providing and paying child support, and may look for a "stable" career.

What is your personal definition of success, and have you achieved it?

Success is personal to each individual. My personal definition is to be able to spend my time where and how I want to spend it, and to know I am making a difference. The difference I believe I am personally here to make is helping people feel free to be themselves, fully, without fear.

I feel like I have achieved success, but I also have goals yet to be attained. You never really arrive if you want to keep growing.

However, if you're busy chasing something that will make you 'successful' only after you attained it, what is the point? If you're not going to love where you are right now, along the journey, that is a problem. So I am enjoying the journey, and I have not arrived.

You must set your intention around your idea of success and what that means to you, according to your personal values. I want to spend time with family, to spend time in nature, to explore other cultures, and in all of the things I do, be a space for people to be free to be themselves. I want to live on a lake, I want to work very hard and focus during certain periods of time, and take lots of vacations as well. Ideally, I will raise a family. I also know I impact families around the country every day through the work I do. I have some of these things already, and I am taking the "one next action" toward the others each day.

What didn't I ask you about that you think is important to convey to other budding and current single women entrepreneurs?

I think there's an interesting notion of feminine and masculine energy in business. Traditional business on the whole tends to be more masculine. By masculine, I mean traditional business is more about having a plan, being in control, thinking things through— an active, dominating energy occurs within it. It tends to be more masculine.

However, there is also feminine energy, which to me is more allowing and flowing. It is airy and allows people (including clients and customers) to flow into your life and form relationships. With the feminine, you have a general plan, but you're following your intuition more. There's a great quote by Einstein that embodies this idea, which is this: "The intuitive mind is a sacred gift and the rational mind is a faithful servant. We have created a society that honors the servant and has forgotten the gift." Our society in recent history has been very rational, very structured and data-based, and that's more masculine energy. I think this economic downturn is telling us that this way of thinking about work and society isn't working anymore.

By Erin Albert

I, personally, think it is a call that we need to bring more feminine energy into the business world. This shift is hard to do. It is hard for me. I am an engineer and a business owner. I have a lot of masculine energy. I actually have to be intentional about bringing in more feminine energy. But it always brings unimagined and unpredicted results.

So I would say, honor your femininity in business. If you're in the corporate world, even as a woman, you might put on a suit and act more masculine in order to fit in and "succeed." However, when you're an entrepreneur, you get to decide to be feminine. You don't have to play a role. When you're in charge, you can be more authentic.

Lastly, I have to say that most quantum leaps occurred in my business when I decided to let go of control. I set an intention about something, and then I walk away from it. I'll go take a bubble bath and the exact idea I need pops into my head when I'm not forcing myself to think about something. Or, maybe I'll go for a walk and leave it alone and then have an epiphany. I think women sometimes have an easier time releasing control and letting the ideas come to them. But we all have stuff that has happened in the past that makes us think we will be safer if we control life. This ruins our results, and our fun. We never really can take control, and we lose access to our intuition when we try. Women may have an advantage because we are a little better at tapping our intuition, and also, it is a little safer for us to follow it. "Women's intuition" is a little more acceptable. Intuitive men feel a little more out of place. I work with both men and women as clients. I'd like to think that it is changing, but for now, women can use that advantage.

Larvetta Loftin

L3 Eventeurs, Limelight Arts Group &
My Kiddie Country Club

Larvetta L. Loftin *is a certified life coach, speaker and visioneer. Her coaching process is to help her clients engineer their visions into reality to attract her model of "Nothing is Impossible." She also provides tools to turn passions into a revenue stream. As you'll see below, Larvetta is also a serial entrepreneur.*

L3 Eventeurs is a full service lifestyle marketing and special events company in Chicago. Founded in 2000, L3 Eventures' marketing architects create award-winning campaigns that focus on attracting brand affinity by building eminent relationships between brands and targeted programs. They specialize in reaching the multi-cultural segment with experiential campaigns, sponsorship negotiation, consumer promotions, branding, graphic design, live media programming, web based campaigns, faith, PR and advertising. Their website is: www.l3eventeurs.com.

Limelight Arts Group promotes and enriches culture in their community by cultivating creativity and imagination. They work to harness theater skills such as voice, body movement and imagination to produce high quality, entertaining and affordable non-musical theatre productions to celebrate the achievements of their local community.

__My Kiddie Country Club__ is a mobile theatre arts company utilizing the arts to spark imagination and discovery in a fun and educational way. Their goal is helping children 9 months to 7 years old adopt ingredients, such as motor skills, social skills, self esteem and independence, which they need to grow to be confident, happy and successful. My Kiddie Country Club also provides themed birthday parties.

Can you describe your businesses in one sentence each?

I have multiple businesses, but I will describe each. I run a lifestyle marketing company, a children's theater company, a not for profit organization, and I'm a certified life coach.

L3 Eventeurs is a full service lifestyle marketing, advertising, PR and events company specializing in building eminent relationships between brands and targeted programs that attract brand affinity and loyalty.

My Kiddie Country Club is a mobile theater arts company that promotes music, theatre, dance and music for children ages 9 months to 7 years of age.

Limelight Arts Group is an organization that promotes the arts and imagination for children and young teens.

And finally, through **Larvetta Loftin Coaching**: as a certified life coach, speaker and visioneer, I help my clients engineer their visions into reality to attract the coaching model of "nothing is impossible."

What advantages do you think you have as a solo business owner that married people don't have?

I certainly have the flexibility and the support system whether it comes from my family or friends to fully engage in my businesses. Having the ability to have this freedom to pursue my dreams is the difference between singles and married people. When you become one in a marriage, you can't make decisions alone. You have to be considerate of your oneness with your spouse. You have to build goals within your marriage, and sometimes those goals supersede your own personal or professional goals.

What about disadvantages?

Certainly, the advantage of being married as an entrepreneur happens when you have someone who you can count on to support you 100% of the time and is your fan. At least, it appears as or is perceived as a sense of security. I don't have this as a single woman, so I view this as a disadvantage.

Do you think business ownership has led you to remain single?

I can answer that as yes and no. Historically, I've always put my business and career first, so the desire to marry wasn't high on my list. Now, I have a significant other. We've been dating for 3 years. It is refreshing to have a partner who does support you one hundred percent. It has allowed for me to share more about my business and be able to connect with my partner. But when it becomes marriage, he's very serious about the fact that we need to be financially secure to be able to handle my dreams as well as his dreams. He's an entrepreneur as well. We are committed to each other, but we realize if we get married, we are committed to the commitment. He believes it is his responsibility to be a provider to the marriage.

So, you attracted another entrepreneur into your life.

Yes. Having dated men who didn't understand the business was very challenging in past relationships and it became stressful. It's good to be connected to another entrepreneur because he understands the lows and the highs; the togetherness of it all is so much greater. I think entrepreneurs attract other entrepreneurs because they are trusting in their faith and both people in the relationship are doing something that each really wants to do. On the flip side, it's challenging, because we are operating under two "TBDs"—or to be determined lives. Entrepreneurs understand the high highs and the low lows, and when you bring two entrepreneurs into a relationship, that understanding makes their bond that much stronger.

What advice would you give another single woman who is thinking about starting a business?

The first thing I would tell any single woman is to write down her vision: have a journal. I am a diary and journal junkie. Writing something down makes it more concrete, or holds an individual more accountable. Second, build a board of directors—get a team that you can share insight with and support your business backbone. You need people who can help you understand contracts, accounting, and even your spiritual self. Get a spiritual advisor, a lawyer and an accountant on your team and let them be your sounding board. Third, be engaged and involved in women's business organizations. Supporting other entrepreneurs is a great way to build your business and make connections. Word of mouth referrals are still a very effective way to build your business, and knowing other people is crucial to building your business. Lastly, I strongly believe you have to not only have a plan, but also have multiple plans in order to build opportunities. If you become the master of your destiny, then you can create unlimited opportunities for yourself. Also, that might mean that you have to take a day job in your field while building your business.

Let's discuss this, because some single women believe a business must be operated only full-time, while others believe in building a business part-time while holding down a day job. What is your philosophy on the part-time versus full-time method of entrepreneurship?

I can only speak from my personal experience. In March 2000, I quit my day job (I was an ad executive for two and a half years) at the highest point in my career, having gained a wonderful reputation in the business. When I quit, I became a consultant. I created a consulting company that focused on reaching the multicultural segment. I took a consulting job for 6-9 months and it was my only stream of income at the time, but I was building contacts and building the company. I have to say that during the course of that contract, I did get the feeling that the client wanted me to become a full-time employee; but honestly, the entrepreneur in me just wasn't looking for a day job.

Your network is your net worth. The more people you have at the table with you, the more opportunities you can get at the table with the people who make decisions. If you are managing a multi-million dollar brand, guess what happens? If you do good work, they'll call you back. That connection becomes invaluable.

Part-time or full-time, if you're going into a business, go in with your whole heart. Sometimes, that means gaining experience with big companies in a day job setting, because a lot of big companies won't bother with small startups. However, if you've done good work for them, your credibility and reputation in a small business might allow you the chance at retaining that client. You have to do the business one hundred percent, but you have to do it on your terms. As a consultant, you still can do it under your own terms. You're still an entrepreneur. And, once you're an entrepreneur, you'll always be an entrepreneur.

What was the best training you received to prepare you as a business owner?

This goes way back, but my dad was an entrepreneur. He made some poor choices. He failed. But he had the ability to think outside the box. So, it was definitely in my lineage. When I was in college, I learned how to take my entrepreneurial spirit to the next level and had a T-shirt business.

My parents didn't go to college. They wanted me to work a 9-5 job and move up the career ladder working for someone else. But I had it inside me to be an entrepreneur. I'm a big idea person AND an action person. Having it in my lineage, it became a method of survival for me in college. It meant freedom. If I made a certain amount of money in my T-shirt business, I didn't have to get a "job."

Single. Women. Entrepreneurs.

Did you take on a partner in any of your businesses at any time?

I've attempted partnerships several times. The first two businesses with partnerships are now closed. The first partnership experience included another woman who was an entrepreneur, and I still had a day job. It became challenging for me because of the day job. I had the opposite situation in the second partnership—the partners had day jobs, but I didn't. The pressure, therefore, was all on me. They brought the capital and I had to invest the time. It was a struggle. Just recently I tried to build a partnership and it just didn't work. A partner must bring contacts, money, or both to a partnership. I made the mistake of trying to partner with someone who couldn't bring either to the company.

How important are your social and personal networks to the success of your business?

Networking is very important, and very significant to the growth and success of a business. I'm a master networker. It is important to be intentional with your networking at events. I make an intent that I'm going to meet four people and make connections.

Making a connection isn't giving someone your business card, however. It's a sincere, "I love your shoes" or "I loved your talk!" conversation. I will say it again—your network is your net worth. I may not have a whole lot, but I have access to people who have a whole lot. When I go to fundraisers, I may not have a lot of money to donate, but I can find 10 people as a crew who can buy a table. You can pull two tables together and guess what? You've become the "go to" person because you can put the groups together.

What else didn't I ask you about you and your business that you wanted me to?

One of the areas that is important to me and that I am personally passionate about is that we need to make more connections in minority communities. Said another way, if you are an African American, how important is connecting with other African American businesses? It is very important, and I don't think we do enough of it. If I'm in Chicago and working in Indianapolis, for example, why can't people form a partnership? I'm working with someone in Detroit to see how we can create a partnership. We need to form a national network of support as minority business owners. That will allow us to partner and drive the economy back. I just wish we could do more of that rather than being constant competitors.

In order to form a national network, I started an organization called Leading Ladies. It is an empowerment women's experience that I will take to other markets and provide women with tools and resources for taking themselves to their next levels of success. There aren't a lot of organizations for women minority business owners, but there are a few organizations that target this area. That's why I created Leading Ladies. Many of the minority organizations don't allow us to fully connect. I'm passionate about Leading Ladies because it is beyond just coming together; it is putting things in motion and having accountability to each other as members. That's what we need in our lives and organizations.

Also, I'm heading up entrepreneurship development in my church. There are not enough resources to help entrepreneurs get started and NOT be intimidated. Startup business owners need a coach, mentor, or someone to help them move forward and be bold and confident. Both boldness and confidence speak success. That is an area that I'm passionate about and want to help other minority women connect with each other.

Sonya Mittelman

The Law Offices of Sonya F. Mittelman

Sonya Mittelman *was born in New York City and has lived there her entire life. She lived with her parents and brother. Her family now is her brother, sister-in-law, niece, and nephew. Both her parents died in 2009. She attended public schools in New York City and graduated from SUNY New Paltz in 1980 and Syracuse Law School in 1983. She was admitted to the New York Bar in 1984, and began practicing law that year, and has been practicing ever since.*

The Law Offices of Sonya F. Mittelman *was established in 2003. They are a full service elder law and estate planning firm in New York. They are dedicated to ensuring the future for their clients, and their clients' loved ones. You can find them on the web at: www.sfmelderlaw.com.*

Can you describe your business in one sentence?
We plan for your life, not your death.

Single. Women. Entrepreneurs.

What advantages do you think you have as a solo business owner that married people don't have? Disadvantages?

The biggest advantage is the ability to schedule my own time without having to account to others. My biggest disadvantage is there is no other source of income for me, and no one else to attend to the household tasks while I'm working and/or away.

Do you think business ownership has led you to remain single?

Possibly. I am not willing to give up time that goes into the business to seek out dates. I also invest my funds in business networking events over singles events. My business is important to me, and I will only date someone who would support that. This may lead to having fewer prospects.

What advice would you give another single woman who is thinking about starting a business?

Decide the relative importance of your business and of dating. The probability is that you will not have the time and/or the money to invest in both. If your business is going to continue to be of importance to you, seek potential dating partners who will support your importance of business ownership.

What about being a single WOMAN business owner?
Do you think it is easier, the same, or harder than being a single man starting a business?

I do not think being a single woman business owner is any different than being a single man or a married woman business owner, as long as being a business owner is as important to you as your martial status. Your business requires time and attention as would another relationship. If the person is willing to give his/her business that attention, s/he will succeed. Gender and martial status neither enable nor disable a person from being an entrepreneur. It is about the individual.

By Erin Albert

So, you're saying that owning a business and investing time in it is much like investing time in a relationship with a significant other or a personal relationship?

Yes. Your business will need you at times just as a human being would. Work/life balance is usually viewed as the less work, the better. That approach will not work for business owners. Our work is part of life, not separate from it. The business's needs must be balanced with other parts of life, but must also be given equal importance.

What was the best training you received to prepare you as a business owner?

I had no training prior to becoming a business owner. I am currently receiving coaching through the Big Fish Nation program. Big Fish Nation is a program for woman business owners, which combines business and life coaching. They can be found on the web at www.bigfishnation.com, or on Facebook. Lorin Beller-Blake, the founder, is also on Twitter (@LorinB).

If you had to start another business, what have you learned that you might do differently—either about yourself, or about how to run a business in general?

I would not do anything differently. What I have learned is that my business is a reflection of me. Just being me is the only thing I can do.

Is your business specifically tailored to a singles market?

No. But there are a number of factors that make my services uniquely important to single people. For example, if a married person without children dies without a will, all of his/her assets go to the spouse. However, if a single person without children dies without a will, assets go first to siblings and then to other relatives, down to first cousins' children. These could be people you might never have even met. New York State has an order of who may make health care decisions for you if you cannot. For married people, that would be the spouse. For the single, it starts with children, and then others. If there is more than one person within a category, confusion may ensue. Also, a single person is less likely to have joint bank accounts with another. In that case, no one may handle his/her financial affairs.

All of this makes it more important for single people to have their own documents in place. Single people are also more likely to be the caregivers for the older generation, because it is believed, often incorrectly, that s/he has more time. This especially can be a problem for single business owners, in a sense that the single business owner caring for elderly parents may be caring for others, just like married people with children do. I can assist my clients with finding alternatives to an individual becoming the sole caregiver.

You lost both your parents in 2009, which had to be difficult. How did those losses change your business, and now, how you serve your clients?

I was always aware that my business has a very human element. I am dealing with human beings at their most vulnerable time. My losses made that even clearer. I was very much a slave to my emotions, as any client would be. This has made me more accommodating to my client's individual needs, including their time factors. I will work weekends, or off-hours, if that makes it easier for them. I will ask questions and make suggestions to ensure that all needs are met in the best way possible for them.

Eldercare is becoming a huge issue now that the baby boomer generation is aging and hitting retirement. You are part of the Eldercare Alliance. Can you share more about how we can all be more proactive about eldercare?

Start early. Too many people do crisis planning. As soon as you see signs the elder may need care, start planning, not just for him or her, but for yourself as well. Figure out what you can do. Consider the needs of your business and others in your life. Do not think you can or even should do it all. I believe we can have it "all" or at least as much as we want, but not all at the same time. Something will give, but only you can decide what that is for you.

Once you are clear on what you can do, you have to have an open and honest communication with your parents and siblings. View the relationships as they are now. Yes, daddy is Superman, and mommy is the most beautiful woman in the world, but that viewpoint is now not helpful. See them and yourself as you are now. Ask yourself, can I spend time with them without needing an escape? With your siblings, the same applies; continuing to worship the older one or treating the "baby" as one is not helpful. Drop the Smothers Brothers' routine of "Maybe mom or dad did like him/her best." That thinking is pointless now. I also recommend the book, *They're Your Parents, Too!* by Francine Russo. This is a helpful guide to how siblings can survive their parents aging without driving each other crazy.

If you are the in-law, walk a fine line. As much as you may consider yourself or even be considered "family," your role is not the same. What made the family what it is today happened long before you came along. What you did or would do may not work. Support your spouse, but also understand that right now, he or she has a role as child/sibling that is separate from you and your relationship. For those who do not have children, there is another issue: the chorus of 'you have more time'. Be prepared to meet the challenge. Be honest with yourself first. Do you think you should do more, and if so, why?

After dealing with your parent(s)' needs, you just become more aware of how soon your own time may come. Start thinking about what you would want. Look into long term care insurance, and get your own legal documents done.

Why do you think more single/divorced and widowed women start more businesses than men in their respective categories, and does your theory match your own rationale for starting a business?

I am not sure why other single women have started businesses, but I started my business after being downsized. I would say that my reason would not have changed had I been married.

What is your personal definition of success, and have you achieved it?

My definition is being able to be self-sufficient and also do something I enjoy—and yes, I have achieved it.

Roxanne Nicolas

Glam Designs, LLC

R oxanne Nicolas *graduated Summa Cum Laude and Phi Beta Kappa from Northwestern University with a degree in economics and has 13 years of combined experience in marketing research and finance. She graduated with High Honors from the University of Chicago Booth School of Business in 2005 with a M.B.A. and concentrations in marketing, entrepreneurship, and organizational behavior, with the goal of starting a fashion-related business and designing her own line of dresses. She has also taken classes through the Fashion Design program at the Illinois Institute of Art-Chicago. After she began ballroom dancing in 2007 and attending local dance competitions, the idea for Glam Designs was born. Officially launched in November 2010, Glam Designs brings together Roxanne's passions for dance and fashion. Roxanne competes in the Pro-Am division as an amateur dancer in the American Smooth and International Latin divisions, wearing her own designs.*

Glam Designs *offers modern, elegant, dance dresses for rent and* *sale. Inspired by evening gowns and cocktail dresses, each one-of-a-kind dress is locally hand made in the Chicago area using high quality materials such as Swarovski rhinestones. They offer dresses in a range of sizes, including dresses for petites and teens. Their dresses are appropriate for a range of dance styles, including but not limited to: ballroom/dancesport, argentine tango, salsa, and swing. In addition to dance competitions, Glam Designs dresses can be worn for dance showcases and performances and beauty pageant talent competitions. Renting a dress from Glam Designs allows every dancer to have a unique dance costume for each competition. Their two-day "Try-On-Rental" service allows you to determine fit and suitability for your next performance. Performance and competition rentals are five days. Glam Designs is available for trunk shows at dance studios or dance camps and events. They will bring a wide selection of dance costumes making it a fun opportunity to try on multiple dance dress styles. For those willing to travel to the Chicago area for dress fittings, they also offer the option of a custom-made dress. Glam Designs also offers a rhinestoning service for those who want to add extra sparkle to their dance shoes or an existing dress. Contact them at: www.glamdesigns.com.*

Can you describe your business in one sentence?

Glam Designs rents and sells modern, elegant, high-quality, one-of-a-kind dance dresses for competitions, showcases, and performances.

Why did you start Glam Designs?

I knew pretty early on after graduating from college that working in corporate America was not a good long-term fit for me. I looked into getting a Ph.D. in Economics so that I could teach at a liberal arts college, but I realized that I did not have the passion for economics that the degree required, so that led me to business school. At that point, I was 26 and I knew I wanted to own my own business. Also, I always loved fashion, and my best friend and I in high school joked we'd own our own dress shop one day. It was fun to think about

160

then, but I never thought about it as more than a daydream. At 26, I asked myself—why couldn't it be reality?

I then began thinking about opening a clothing boutique, and decided to go to business school so I could learn how to run my own business. I took a lot of marketing and entrepreneurship classes (I originally was an economics major in undergrad), and had worked primarily in finance. After business school, I realized that instead of selling other designers' clothes, it would be more fun and rewarding to design the clothes myself. So, I decided to go to design school. I took design classes for 2 years and learned the fundamentals of design. I finally learned how to sew, make patterns, and do basic draping. Around the time I started design school, I began taking ballroom dancing lessons. It didn't take long before I was completely hooked. I began attending local dance competitions and eventually started competing myself. I started noticing what other women were wearing at those competitions and I realized that specializing in dance dresses would be a great fit for me, because it gave me the chance to marry my passions for both dance and design. So I started the business, initially making the dresses from scratch myself. Eventually, I found a pattern maker and a seamstress that I now work with and put together my first collection of thirty dresses. Having them work on the pattern making, sewing and embellishment has left me to work on the business side. I officially launched my website the first week of November, 2010.

What advantages do you think you have as a solo business owner that married people don't have?

I think from a time perspective, I have more flexibility, because I don't have the responsibility of children or a significant other. Because I'm single, I can set my own schedule. It is easier to plan a timeline and schedule meetings with people, and if I have to be up late to work through something, I can.

What about disadvantages?

I guess I really haven't seen any yet. If I need feedback, I bounce ideas off of my friends or my brother—people I trust. Whenever I've needed ideas or feedback, I've been lucky enough to find those resources.

Do you think business ownership has led you to remain single?

I don't think business ownership has affected me one way or the other, because being married is not something I've focused on. Whether or not I started this business, I would approach relationships the same way. Undoubtedly, I don't have much free time right now because I am juggling my corporate job, this business, and my dancing. But even if I had more free time, I would not put more effort into meeting someone than I currently am. I just have a very laid-back attitude with respect to relationships. I've learned through experience that if a relationship or marriage is meant to happen, it will happen. You can't force it. But if I happened to meet the right person, I would find the time for a relationship.

What advice would you give another single woman who is thinking about starting a business?

My ultimate goal is to make this business my full-time job, but right now the income from my corporate job is funding my small business, so it is necessary to continue working while building a client base. I would suggest to someone that if they can continue to work their day job while starting a business without it negatively impacting either, I would continue working for the time being. Secondly, it's definitely important to learn how to multi-task and prioritize. "Triage" is the word I use to describe how I approach decision making. What absolutely needs to be done at this moment to keep things moving along? You must be able to be decisive and make decisions in a short time frame. If my day job requires me to get a project out the door today, that is what I focus on today. You have to be flexible and learn to adapt to the situation at hand.

A few weeks ago I had a last minute opportunity to be a vendor at a local fundraiser and only had a couple of days to produce marketing materials for that, so I made the time to develop information for that event. I've become very good at prioritizing for my day job, my dancing, and my small business. I've also had to learn how to see the big picture. While it's important to be detail oriented, you also have to be able to see things from a more global perspective. I can't get the 100 things on my to-do list done in one moment, but which items will have the biggest impact today on helping make my business a success? I've also had to learn to stop being a perfectionist. While it's important to be thorough, there is a point where you hit diminishing marginal returns. In addition, while starting a business is undoubtedly a lot of work, you should not push yourself to the point where it starts to negatively affect your health. I am a very goal-oriented person and I wanted to start this business as quickly as possible. But I was starting to wear myself out to the point that my allergies were really affecting my daily productivity and I was getting chronic sinus infections. You just have to listen to your body and know when to take a break.

Furthermore, I would advise her to hire individuals, contractors, or outsource whatever makes sense, given the amount she has to invest. You do not have to do it all. I started out making my dresses from start to finish. Then I realized my time would be more effectively used finding experts who could help me with the patternmaking and sewing, while I focused on the designing and business end. Lastly, my advice would be not to beat yourself up over any mistakes you make while starting out. Use those mistakes as a learning opportunity and move on.

You're a full-time employee and a part-time entrepreneur. Do you think entrepreneurship leads you to being a better employee?

I do. Business ownership forces me to think about the big picture and that applies to my day job as well. I'm always thinking about the processes here at my corporate job and how they can be improved. Also, because I am juggling several things at once, it has forced me to be as efficient as possible in both my day job and in my business in order to optimize my time.

What about being a single WOMAN business owner? Have you perceived any advantages or disadvantages?

I don't think I've been treated differently by anyone who I've tried to contact thus far because I'm a woman. Some suppliers have been a little difficult to work with, but I'm not sure if that's because I'm female or if that's just the way they treat all their customers. I think that given the type of business I've chosen to go into, there's probably an advantage to being a female dancer in that I understand how these dresses must be functional and comfortable in addition to being beautiful. I serve as my own fit model for many of the dresses to ensure that they stay in place while dancing. As a woman, I can also act as my own advertisement because I can wear my own dresses.

What was the best training you received to prepare you as a business owner?

As it relates to my specific type of business, some of the best advice I've received is from individuals with industry specific knowledge. One of my closest friends was once a costume designer who also did custom design for clients. Hearing about how she dealt with certain client-related situations and getting her opinion on some of the client-related issues I have been dealing with has been very valuable.

The seamstress that I've been working with has also become a friend and mentor. She is self-employed and besides working on projects for clients like myself, she designs and sells her own accessories and knitwear, so she's learned a lot from working with clients over the years. I've really benefited from her sharing her stories and knowledge with me. In business school, I learned an entirely different skill set. Now, for example, I can apply the 4Ps to the marketing of my business. So, while business school gave me a very high level of knowledge in running a business, it is also great to have the support of individuals with industry specific knowledge.

Your business as you mentioned is part-time. Why?

My business is currently a part-time venture while I build a client base. I envision leaving my day job when there's enough momentum to cover my basic living expenses, which I'm hoping occurs by February 2012. The year 2011 will be the year for me to get my name out there. At this point, I have a business and product, but few people know that I exist. Also, for what I am selling, the business will grow by word of mouth. It will spread by the initial few that take a chance on my business. I will focus on local dance studios and pound the pavement via trunk shows, local competitions and events. I also need to think about using search engine optimization and social media to bring brand awareness to a larger audience via the internet. I can still manage everything, but if I get busy with my business, it will definitely be the time for me to say goodbye to my day job.

Did you ever consider taking on a business partner?

I never considered it initially. Now, I divide the business into the creative and business aspects of it. Because of my background I feel I can do both, but it would be nice to have someone else to take care of the business tasks and bounce ideas off, so I can focus on the creative part of the business, which is really the part I find the most fun and rewarding. I would be open to having a partner in the business, provided that we share the same vision for the company's future and have compatible work styles and ethics.

If you had to start another business, what have you learned that you might do differently—either about yourself, or about how to run a business in general?

I've had to learn not to take things personally. Each dress that I design is like a little piece of me. But I understand that everyone has their own sense of style and my dresses are not to everyone's taste. It's interesting because several people have been quick to offer their negative opinion, even when it was not solicited, and it can be hard not to be hurt by that. But I know that you can't please everyone, and I've had to learn to just stay true to who I am and what I like to design. Now I just let any negative comments roll off my back.

Did you start your business with your own capital? Did you try to obtain capital from other sources?

I started with my own capital. I never thought about venture capital because I had heard that they don't provide money to fashion-related start-ups without any experience. In terms of a business loan, this business doesn't require a lot of capital at once. This year, I've been spending money on it little pieces at a time. I prefer using my own money rather than taking out a loan. I just didn't want to be in "debt" if I had the savings and the income to cover my business expenses.

What is your personal definition of success, and have you achieved it?

I think success is being true to who you are and living your life the way you want to live it, regardless of what anyone else may think. It's about living a life of action and not being afraid to go after your dreams. It's about achieving the goals that I set for myself. I usually try to set small goals, each one building on the last. Even though I like having goals, I look at life in general as a journey, a learning experience, and a process rather than just endpoints. Looking back, three and a half years ago, I didn't even know how to sew. Now I have a small design business and make dresses with my own hands! If I give myself another three and a half years, who knows where I'll be?

What has surprised you about launching your business?

I guess the one thing that has really surprised me is that although my day job does take a significant amount of my time, I can still accomplish a lot in addition to it. It took me 8-9 months to create my first collection of 30 dresses. I'm still financially stable and it was worth the time to start my collection. If I had quit my day job to pursue developing my collection, I don't really think I would have gained that much more time. My day job is not always a 9-5 job, either, and between my small business and my corporate job, I work 6-7 days a week. When I'm not working at the day job I am working on my business and pursuing my passion with dance. I feel as long as I continue to make good progress on the small business while working my corporate job, doing everything is still worth it.

And what about 5 years from now? Where do you want to be?

I'm hoping this business will be a successful national or even international business. There are a lot of dancers in Europe, Canada, and Asia. I hope as well that this will be my full-time job and it won't just be me—I will have employees and the business will continue to grow, potentially in directions outside of the dance community. In 5 years, I hope that it will be a viable, profitable, full-time career for me.

Colleen Patterson

TCB Solutions USA, LLC

Originally from Colorado, **Colleen Patterson** *initially moved to Indiana to attend college at Indiana University. She graduated with a degree in Operations & Systems Management. Colleen then worked as a computer programmer for 8 years after she graduated from college. She has two children. When her youngest child attended first grade, she began working outside the home again. She has worked in technology (software and hardware) sales, customer service as a supervisor, and sales and installation of point of sale systems. Colleen has lived in Carmel, Indiana, for the past 16 years. She was married for 22 years and has been single for the past 3 years.*

TCB Solutions USA works with business owners to identify the best solutions for their business challenges and has the processes and resources to systematically increase revenue and decrease expenses. Business owners balance the joys of independence with the frustration of financial uncertainty. They balance the pride of ownership with the risk of overworking. And they also balance attention to detail with the stress of getting everything done. TCB Solutions helps business owners leverage their time and resources to get better results. The company's comprehensive Business Analysis will give business owners the opportunity to talk about their business, how they run the business, and how they feel about running the business. What goals and challenges they have faced in the past, how they are planning for the future development of their business and what they love most about running this business are all part of TCB Solution's analysis. They are online at: www.tcbsolutions-usa.com.

Can you describe your business in one sentence?

My business changes the way small businesses succeed by providing back office support and the processes to systematically increase revenue, decrease expenses and develop and maintain customers.

What advantages and disadvantages do you think you have as a solo business owner that married people don't have?

I don't have a Plan B. And because I don't have a Plan B (in the form of a husband or significant other who contributes to the household income), I have to work harder. By the same token, everything I have now is mine because I've worked for it. One of the best accomplishments is being able to own my own home. Why? Because it is mine! I don't have to worry about pleasing somebody who might disagree with my choices ... no one else has to agree. I reap all the rewards, but I also bear all the risk. This is all up to me.

It has opened me up to the possibility of failure, too. If you're an employee, at times, you might do just the minimum to "get by;" to not fail. As an entrepreneur, sometimes you have to fail in order to succeed. By that, I mean you have to take risks; risks don't always do well—but failures are learning opportunities. Relative to disadvantages, I've been in business now for a year, and I've noticed that I don't have the camaraderie that you get by being in an office environment. You don't have the chance to chat about the Colts game, the holidays, etc. I do miss that. I miss the safety of a Plan B and the camaraderie with the people you're going to see every day.

By Erin Albert

Do you think business ownership has led you to remain single?

Absolutely, I'm still single because I'm not in a place where I'm meeting single men. Hey, do you know any good ones? In my age group, it's hard to find a single man who doesn't have a very good reason for being single. Being a single woman business owner perpetuates my singlehood because I can always find work to do, so even if I can't find a date, I am at least always busy.

What advice would you give another single woman who is thinking about starting a business?

Make sure you have a very good mentor. One thing that helped me significantly was finding someone I trust as a business advisor and who can keep me on the right track. Find someone who has similar values; who can be very honest with you when needed and who is truly interested in helping you accomplish your goals. The mentor doesn't need to be in the same type of business that you're in, either—just someone you can trust, someone who will listen, and someone who you can bounce ideas off of from time to time.

What about being a single WOMAN business owner?

I think being a woman business owner—and a blonde woman business owner—is a disadvantage sometimes because some men fail to take me seriously. I actually do know what I'm talking about, and can help them find the best solutions to help their business flourish. I find that other women business owners—single or not—empathize with my struggles and my successes.

What was the best training you received to prepare you as a business owner?

I took a class from Crystal Synergies on how to network effectively. It wasn't so much the class, (I did learn a lot) but instead, it was the contacts I made in that class that were phenomenal. I took this class to learn how to become a more effective salesperson and interestingly, the people I met in that class had the same business philosophy. I'm actually in business with the people I met in that class. They've been extremely helpful for promoting Create Business Bliss (www.createbusinessbliss.com). The classes were beneficial, but the relationships were priceless.

Did you, or are you running your business as a part-time or full-time venture? Why?

Full-time. In the past year that I've owned my business, I worked in it part-time for the first nine months, then for the last three months have been working in it full-time. The tipping point came when I realized that by working in two different businesses, I was not contributing what I needed to either business to be truly successful. I needed to focus on just one thing. I weighed the pros and cons of both businesses, asking myself which would make me the most satisfied, both in terms of the work and income, and decided it was distributing Create Business Bliss full-time. I just had too many balls in the air while working part-time in two businesses and it wasn't a good fit for me. I needed to focus on one thing—what I'm doing now, to actually become successful.

Did you take on a partner in your business at any time?

Yes. My business partner is also my mentor. Our locations are different. He's in Arizona and I'm in Indiana. We compare notes on the different perspectives of how businesses work in the Southwest versus the Midwest. His background and experiences are really helpful to me. He taught me where to focus, how to incorporate, etc. We are like a well-oiled machine when we work together; we think very much alike.

If you had to start another business tomorrow, what have you learned that you might do differently—either about yourself, or about how to run a business in general?

I really think the biggest thing I learned is to focus on one business. I thought I could do 2-3 things at the same time, but I really ended up not being able to do any of them well. If I was going to start another business, I would definitely decide what it was that I was really going to do and totally focus on it. Decide what you're really personally passionate about. What are you going to do? Do it whole-heartedly.

Did you start your business with your own capital?

I started it with my own capital. I didn't really look at borrowing capital. I knew lots of people who could give out capital. For me, I didn't need it, but if I did, I now know exactly where to go.

Why do you think more single/divorced and widowed women start more businesses than men in their respective categories?

Single women are not afraid of the work involved in starting a business. When I was married, I worked in a full-time job, came home, cleaned, made dinner, and made sure that all schedules were coordinated, homework was finished, etc., while my ex-husband came home, ate dinner and watched TV. Women are already doing most of the work anyway! Don't get me wrong; he worked hard at his job, but so did I. It would have been nice to come home and not have to do another thing. I came home to job number two: wife and mommy.

What is your personal definition of success, and have you achieved it?

My personal definition depends upon what area of my life you're asking about. As far as raising my children, I have definitely succeeded. They are really awesome young adults. In business, I have not quite succeeded, YET, but give me a minute! When I get to the point where my business basically runs itself without me having to be there every minute, I would consider that successful. If I wanted to go to Tonga for a month, for example, I could leave and the business could run without me—that would be success.

Anything else in closing?

One of the things that made me really proud is that my kids DO see how hard I work and they appreciate it. I live in the land of plenty (Carmel, Indiana) and I'm proud of the fact that my kids appreciate what I do for them because they see how hard I work for us. It's an awesome blessing. At a time when I hadn't fully started my business and was not working at a corporate job, I went into friends' houses and cleaned and organized for them, and the kids saw that their mom was willing to do whatever it took to pay the bills. I know that this has rubbed off on my kids. My son works now and goes to school and he NEVER wants to be late. He doesn't take breaks at work. My daughter is at IU studying pre-med, and over the summer she enrolled in a Chinese immersion program, giving up her summer between her senior year in high school and first year of college to continue learning Chinese. She's been asked to reapply for the upcoming summer. Both of my kids are very hard workers and responsible.

My adage is that if I don't sell, I don't eat. But I don't own my own business for the money. I'm helping other business owners grow their businesses. I love the fact that I lend a hand in small business owners becoming more successful, and that is what truly makes me happy.

Peggy Paul

SheTaxi

Peggy **Paul** is the Founder and Visionary of SheTaxi. com. She has an accomplished reputation for start-ups, expansions and organizations in need of change. Through her career, she's raised millions of dollars for charities and inspired thousands to volunteer and give back to their communities. Peggy received numerous national and local awards for her work in the corporate and nonprofit sectors. Peggy believes that life is too short to not do what you love. With SheTaxi, Peggy brings women together to support and mentor each other and discard behaviors of judgment and criticism. She is passionate about tackling ideas about body image and media messaging to women and talking openly about subjects that affect women, but get little attention. Peggy wants women to think differently about themselves and others by moving toward acceptance. She believes that all women, because we are women, should be a community that works to enhance each other.

Single. Women. Entrepreneurs.

SheTaxi is an online vehicle for women who are ready to say goodbye to airbrushing and impossible ideals and hello to content that matters. Compassionate, lively, funny and frank, it's a come-as-you-are community that connects you with friends you just haven't met yet. SheTaxi is at: www.shetaxi.com.

Can you describe your business in one sentence?

SheTaxi is an online vehicle for women to share, connect, laugh and learn.

Where did the idea come from for you to start your business?

It is a little bit of a long story. A few years ago, I had thyroid cancer. Luckily, it was the most curable type of cancer and with the experience, I began assessing my life. First, I looked at my path—who was I? Did my personal values fit my lifestyle? Second, I began to seek out wellness communities online, but I kept finding advertisements for "how to look younger" products and how to make your butt look 10 pounds smaller. I found that contradictory advertising for a well-being site.

Also, I kept seeing the pattern of media focusing on gossip, fashion and Hollywood. What messages are given to women by focusing on these areas? How can a woman achieve well being when they are constantly told they should look differently? Finally, I noticed between TV and online media that women tend to be perceived as competitive, critical of each other and petty. All this information together led me to the desire to build a community online for women to connect with other women and talk about REAL issues and topics. Also, I wanted to provide a portal by which women could talk about ALL the roles of our lives and view women holistically, rather than just their stereotypes. SheTaxi focuses on the whole woman. I also discovered that I wanted flexibility in my own life and work hours that I wanted to work, instead of sitting at a desk for 10 hours a day.

In part of my research of the web, there was quite an array of websites for PARTS of a woman's life. There were sites for women in business, but that was the only thing the site focused on. There were other sites for moms, but if you weren't a mom, you really couldn't relate. For single women (straight or gay), what was available was only about dating and finding "the one;" it was never about being happy as and by yourself. For me, I'm a business owner, but I'm so much more: I'm also a daughter, a friend, a sister, etc., and the media does a wonderful job of labeling people and putting them in one bucket.

My goal with SheTaxi is that you're not coming to the site because you're a single woman who is seeking dating advice, you're coming there for all aspects of your life for support. I found this an issue particularly with the mom sites. We have a motherhood category, but it's about her as a woman, NOT about the kids. How she feels about being a mom is explored. It's about her in that role, not about the children.

Why did you decide on a business geared only towards women?

I am tired of the media messaging to women, which includes the perpetuation of a superficial culture and the false ideals of Hollywood. This has resulted in an epidemic of poor body image and lack of self-acceptance among women. There's a lot of pain out there, and I think a way to solve these social ills is to provide women with a better way of relating and connecting to each other in a more authentic way.

How did the role of thyroid cancer make you discover your calling as an entrepreneur?

In 2004, they found the cancer late in the year. In 2005 while I was recovering, I thought about doing consulting, but the major factor holding me back was health care. I could not get coverage because of the thyroid cancer. Because of that, I went back to work as an employee, but, did keep the idea of my own business in the back of my head.

Recently, I went off COBRA and I'm still faced with health care companies turning me down; they want me cancer free for 7 years. In Minnesota where I live, they do offer health insurance to people who are denied coverage, but the premiums are 25% higher. Honestly, I think a lot of people don't start businesses BECAUSE of the health care problem. I think we have a lot to learn from other countries about health care and costs. When I get to the point of wanting to hire staff, I have to think about insurance costs and it is daunting thinking about that expense. It steers me in the direction of having contractors.

What advantages do you think you have as a single business owner over married business owners?

I think one aspect is flexibility. I don't have accountability to an individual or partner. I can make my own schedule and work when I want to. Second, I have the drive to know that I have to support myself and provide income. I view it as an advantage because I'm not relying on other people to support me financially.

What about disadvantages?

Having a second income is a luxury. When I was interviewing entrepreneurs before I started my own initiative, I noticed that all of them had health care insurance with their spouses. Health insurance is a large expense and holds individuals back from venturing out on their own. Another disadvantage being solo is that I don't have a partner who runs errands, does laundry, pays bills or helps clean the house. I have to tackle that myself. I think a significant other might balance out your life a bit more. Having that partner to do things with that are unrelated to the business is good for the mind and soul. And, having that support and a dedicated ear on your journey would be nice too.

Do you think business ownership has led you to remain single?

Being single, I don't think it necessarily has, but what it does, though—being in the startup stage—is limit my time. At the end of the day, I'm tired, so I don't necessarily have the energy to develop new relationships. It impacts my lifestyle, even in spending time with friends. I only have so much energy to go around. I'm currently dating someone; it's a long distance relationship, and it works for us. I'm in no hurry to be married. It isn't the "everything" to me, nor for a lot of other women.

Did you attract another entrepreneur in your significant other?
No, he is not an entrepreneur. However, he is a CPA for a large healthcare provider (ironically, given my health insurance woes), and he DOES complement my weakness, finances. He is a great financial sounding board for the business and a great balance to my personality. He is a big believer in work/life balance and that helps me when we are together. I tend to forget about my Blackberry more when he's around.

What about being a single WOMAN business owner?
Do you think it is easier, the same, or harder than being a
single man starting a business?
I think women are natural collaborators and relationship builders—that's a HUGE advantage. People and women especially are always willing to help me out. With men, it's a little tougher to do. Women can do this more easily than a man can, and women also do a better job of asking for help.

What was the best training you received to prepare you as a
business owner?
I had a lot of good training. My background is predominantly in corporate philanthropy. I created programs within companies from the ground up, so I had to do business plans, strategic planning, marketing, budgeting, etc. The fortunate part was having the deep pockets of the company, but it also gave me great exposure on how to start a business. I learned through my corporate experience, who is a good hire? I also learned how to let employees go. I learned how to pitch my case to executives and develop business strategies for my department. I was really lucky to have that kind of experience in a corporate setting. That's not always the case that you can literally create a business within a business. When I was young, I was a good

creator and developer. I get bored when things are "managed;" that's not appealing to me at all. I'd rather fight the start-up challenges, take the risks and have constant change and evolution in my work.

Did you, or are you running your business as a part-time or full-time venture? Why?

Full-time. I think the timing of my business made a full-time venture right for me, because I had employment benefits remaining, despite being laid off. I took it as a sign that it was my time to go for it. I had a good grace period to study and foster the idea. Even thinking about the realization of my benefits now ending, I think if I went back to work even on a part-time basis, my energy to drive this business and do what I'm doing right now could be diffused. I could lose momentum. I need to keep forging ahead with this. The passion around it keeps me focused on my vision, and I don't see anything else beyond that at this point in time. It would be difficult for me to work for someone else.

Did you take on a partner in your business at any time?

It's all me. I have no interest in having a partner at all. I considered it, but I have a team I work with, and no one has the vision or passion as I do.

If you had to start another business, what have you learned that you might do differently—either about yourself, or about how to run a business in general?

I have learned to be patient. Things do not go as fast as I think they'll go. Patience has been something I continually try to master. I've also become flexible. You can plan and plan and plan and then a wrench gets thrown into the mix. I can't control everything. I have to "roll with it" and make the most of every situation.

Recently, I put an advisory group together—my "board of directors." Even though SheTaxi is less than a year old, I wish I had done that sooner. I was getting burned out and needed a sounding board and outside eyes to look at the business. At our first meeting the amount of clarity they provided in their feedback was invaluable. I think I cried for half of the meeting from exhaustion and thankfulness for them standing by the business and me.

I have some items on my to-do list that moved week-to-week and then month-to-month. I learned that those are signs of my weak areas. The longer they sit on my to-do list, the more apparent it is that I need someone else to do them. Or I need to suck it up and do them. Having a resource to support my weak areas is important and then it frees my mind from that guilty energy.

I've been fortunate to have a team of young female interns helping me on this journey. At times I have forgotten their age and minimal work experience and let them forge ahead too soon without the proper training. I realize this needs to be a priority for me to take the extra time to work with them and provide more guidance and direction. My interns are smart, eager and loyal employees. I wouldn't be where I am today without them.

Is your business specifically tailored to a singles market?

In some areas of our content online, we do focus on shedding light on what it is really like to be a single in a couple's world. We also look at the transition of divorce and learning how to live solo again and what an adjustment that can be. We've also looked at the lack of understanding between solos and marrieds. Married people make assumptions that solos are living an exciting life, and then the solos make an assumption that marrieds are too busy with their spouses and/or kids. Therefore, we discuss how these communities can really divide. For example, in my prior relationship, I had a group of "couple" friends for dinner parties. But, when that relationship ended, my invitations did too.

Also, women need to be happy by themselves, and they don't necessarily have to have a partner in order to be happy. When you're happy as a single, you're a much better partner. There are societal pressures associated with being solo. People have been trying to marry me off for years. These are the types of issues we explore on SheTaxi.

Single. Women. Entrepreneurs.

How important were mentors in your entrepreneurial career?

Mentoring goes back to a lot of exposure I had during my corporate career. I had some great mentors who pushed and challenged me. They made me spread my wings, reach and then exceed outrageous goals. I am grateful for their mentorship.

Did you start your business with your own capital?

I used some of my own capital and I have one investor—my mother. I love my mom! I just need to pay her back. When I was laid off and unemployed, I was NOT a candidate for a loan because I was not viable. Fortunately, the interest rate I am paying my "investor" back is higher than what any bank can offer her. So it is a win-win on both sides.

How important are your social and personal networks to the success of your business?

It is everything. Especially the social network. That tends to be friend based. If you have flat, skeptical, negative people around you, that will hinder you. You have to have a good support system. I have learned a lot about some of my friendships and who stands by me. Sadly, I think a few friends are jealous of my endeavor and of my fulfillment launching my business. I try to stay away from the energy vampires and surround myself with people who are on the same path as I am.

What is your personal definition of success, and have you achieved it?

This is a hard question. I equate success with self-satisfaction. If I am happy, challenged, having some fun and helping out my community, that is satisfying. Having healthy and thriving relationships with friends and family add to that as well. And if the income follows, even better. That's success to me. Even now, I don't have the monetary return yet, but I feel really good about where I'm at and I'm on a good path!

By Erin Albert

What are your personal values, and how do they fit into your career and your company?

Values are very important. With the corporate culture, for example, I worked for a company that had great values and standards, but the more people they added in the mix, the harder it became to run their company based upon values. Most recently, I worked at an ad agency, which had a culture about fun, playing hard and working hard and most people who worked there loved it. However, the bigger you get, the harder it is to maintain that momentum. Businesses eventually come down to the bottom line.

For me, I started working on my values for SheTaxi from the beginning. I want people working for SheTaxi to have fun, be kind, be respectful and communicative. It is also important that we support our communities through time and money. We may only have time now, but, eventually we'll have the money to share. My goal is to have everyone who is working for SheTaxi LOVING what they do, no matter what that is for them. I believe you can have a healthy and thriving work environment if you hire people who are authentic and real and the leader(s) exude those qualities as well.

What's your 10-year vision for SheTaxi?

SheTaxi will be the leading social networking site for women. We'll quickly evolve to in-person events and workshops that will be held throughout the globe. Team Taxi will serve as a cadre of resources for topics related to women. I envision a storefront at the Mall of America (in Minneapolis) where women can take a break from shopping and put their feet up, have a cup of tea, meet the team and listen to a podcast about topics they care about. The brand is about improving women's lives and moving them forward.

Is there any advice you would give to a novice entrepreneur?

There's a loneliness factor for entrepreneurs, especially for single entrepreneurs. All day, every day, you are the "go to" guy! But there come times when it would be nice for someone else to please answer the question than just me.

You also feel tremendous pressure from people looking to you to keep something going. At times it feels like nothing will get done unless I start it, direct it or do it. I'm the one with the vision.

I put together a strategic team or board of advisors a month ago, and at that first meeting as I shared previously, I cried during half of it because I was so exhausted. They gave me fantastic advice, which I took, and which was to get my business out of my house and get away from it at the end of the day. Hearing that from someone else was helpful because it was validating and exactly what I needed. It was great to finally have someone who I could voice my ideas to and share information on the company, because I hadn't yet shared these ideas with anyone! It was one of the ways around the loneliness factor for me.

Also, you have to believe in yourself. If you don't, you won't succeed. When the chips are down and it's only up to you to forge ahead, you have to know that you can when the rough days come along.

Tasha Phelps

Phelco Technologies, Inc.

Tasha Phelps *is the President & CEO of Phelco Technologies, Inc., a company that she formed in 1997. Tasha believes that a major contribution to the success of the company has been her vast experience in using technology to manage information.*

Tasha is driven by four areas of concern: 1. Minority and Women-owned business development, 2. Education, 3. Access to information and 4. Political reform. As an active member of the National Association of Women Business Owners, and the Greater Indianapolis Chamber Education & Workforce Task Force, Tasha is committed to building a stronger workforce through training. As a part of her commitment to the community, Tasha even published a cookbook, Dinners and Desserts, *to be used to benefit charitable initiatives. The book can be purchased online at the following site: www.phelco.com/ladybug/bookstore.htm.*

As a 2009 Indiana Commission for Women Torchbearer Recipient, a 2008 Indy's Best & Brightest (Alum), a 2007 Forty under 40 winner, and the 2009 Recipient of the Mayor's Diversity in Business, Tasha believes it's all about strategy. Being able to FIRST understand the nature of an issue, followed with the capacity to RESOLVE it, has created a competitive advantage for herself and for her company. Tasha is quick to share her entrepreneurial perspective as an industry educator, a youth mentor and a business owner, because, she believes that, "Simply being exposed to information and opportunity, creates a stronger perspective to handle an issue."

Phelco Technologies, Inc., is an infrastructure delivery firm in central Indiana, that carries multiple certifications—MBE, WBE, DBE, ACDBE, 8(a) and SDB. Phelco clearly defines e-business as the strategic (and secure) integration of technology into any given business model. This has become the company's core competency and has led to more than 13 years of profitability. The company's key service areas of technology include: IT infrastructure design and installation, IT security, emergency preparedness planning, business impact analysis, web development, data management, IT staff augmentation, Dell solutions and general IT consulting. By developing powerful strategies for communication between IT and management departments, Phelco is able to achieve process-driven solutions. Learn more at: www.phelco.com.

What advantages do you think you have as a solo business owner that married people don't have?

If I claim any "advantages" it would be the SAME as the disadvantages. The (so called) "advantage" in not having a spouse is that I don't have to negotiate my plans. If I want to do something, I just simply do it, without compromise to anyone else.

What about disadvantages?

That I don't have anyone to *lean* on or "debrief" with when I get home ... there's no one at home to hug me after a long day. Beyond that, there's no one at home to help share the responsibilities of the "home" life.

By Erin Albert

Do you think business ownership has led you to remain single?

Yes, to some degree, because of the simple fact, (I believe), that not many men understand my drive. I'm told that my drive is potentially something they would have to compete with in order to have my time.

What advice would you give another single woman who is thinking about starting a business?

Three things: First that it TRULY is imperative that the drive and passion exist internally. Second, to have a strong understanding of work/life balance in order to stay sane. Third, that one should be prepared for "resistance" in emotional assistance from friends and family. If there are no other entrepreneurs in the family (or extended family), it's likely that no one will (truly) understand the rollercoaster ride or the late hours that come with being a business owner.

Do you think there are advantages/disadvantages to being a single business owner? Do you think it is harder, or easier?

Yes, there are advantages AND disadvantages. Whether it is harder or easier is contingent on every individual. Not every experience is the same, and not every definition of "advantages and disadvantages" is the same.

For me, it has been an advantage that I'm a single mom. I've been able to stay focused on the most important task in my life (being a mother) and I've been able to pursue my personal passions in the development and growth of Phelco (my business). I also believe that having Multiple Sclerosis (MS) is an advantage in my favor. I am THANKFUL that I have MS and many (if not most) people look at me as crazy when I make that statement. Because I have been "chosen" to bear this illness, I think it has given me a different perspective on life. I feel that I am able to help others overcome (their own) personal challenges and situations they may deem as "disadvantages."

Single. Women. Entrepreneurs.

What was the best training you received to prepare you as a business owner?

I've ALWAYS known that I would work for myself. It was never really a question for me. Truly, I never grew up thinking about "What my ideal job might be" or "Where I'd like to work." It was more like, "What kind of business would I start?" or "Did I want to travel to have to see my clients?" When I was a small child (I'm told around 4 years old), I used to create and build board games to amuse myself. I was always trying to create the new "fad" and sell it. I remember asking my mom to take me to the store so that I could get some cinnamon extract. I wanted to make (and sell) cinnamon toothpicks! (I recall I was only in second grade). I remember selling sodas at garage sales, etc. Long story, short, I was never idle.

Did you, or are you running your business as a part-time or full-time venture? Why?

Full-time. It used to be "just me" and then DIVINE INTERVENTION took over and led me on a path that inevitably grew my business and gave me legs to hire others! The 'tipping point' was when I was awarded a contract that pushed (if not forced) me to hire help. From that point on, I haven't looked back, and it has been steady growth.

Did you take on a partner in your business at any time?

No, I have no partners and don't really have any desire to have them. I once *tried* to merge my business with another because we had complimentary services to offer and (I thought at the time) a credible professional relationship. As it turned out, that was not the case, and I'm thankful that I nixed the deal before it was complete.

If you had to start another business, what have you learned that you might do differently—either about yourself, or about how to run a business in general?

The partnership question above was something I would do differently. But at the end of the day, I've learned that PASSION is what drives successful entrepreneurship, and if none exists, the likelihood of the business gaining ground is small. The passion has to burn from within the individual starting the business.

Friends and family might not always understand this passion either—the idea that sometimes as a business owner, you might have to work on a holiday or into the night. Even on vacation, I call them a "vacawork," because my mind is always on the business— looking for and creating opportunities, especially in this current economic environment. I'm always looking for the opportunity. Economic challenges ignite that opportunistic outlook.

How important were mentors in your entrepreneurial career?

Very. Mentors for me were and are my professional parents. Some 'kick me in the tail' when I'm not performing as I should, others function as cheerleaders, continuing to encourage me that I CAN do what I've been positioned to do.

Did you start your business with your own capital?

I started with my own capital, and no, I did not try to obtain capital from other sources.

How important are your social and personal networks to the success of your business?

For me, they are essentially one and the same. The only exception would be my PARENTAL/extended family dynamic. That, I keep separate, and yes, it is HIGHEST on my priority list.

Why do you keep your family network separate?

I keep them separate (for the most part) because they exist in my "personal space." Though I am (professionally) an open book, I don't let everyone see me in my personal space. I think it's what keeps me balanced and humble. I know where/what my reality is, and I know how to "perform" in my professional space.

Single. Women. Entrepreneurs.

Why do you think more single/divorced and widowed women start more businesses than men in their respective categories, and does your theory match your own rationale for starting a business?

I've never been married, so I can't compare my rationale against that of others. I think (in general) single women who are "career-focused" are more likely to go the entrepreneurial route because of an inherent characteristic of independence. If I was to make a conclusion/assumption, I would speculate that independent women in relationships will ultimately find a path of entrepreneurship that will blend easily with their lifestyles.

What is your personal definition of success, and have you achieved it?

My personal definition of success is being able to "be me" and "put food on the table while I'm being me." Using that definition, yes, I believe that the combination of:

1. My medical condition (MS)
2. Being a single mother
3. Being a minority

all lend favorably to my commitment to my own personal success.

Has it been a challenge being a single mom, business owner, and someone managing a chronic illness?

It has only been since 2008 that I've begun to "come out of the shadows" and talk openly about my MS. I was ashamed, and I didn't know how others would react. I was scared that people would be afraid to be around me because it isn't (necessarily) a very "well-known" condition. The biggest challenge over the last decade for me has been to understand my limitations. First I had to accept them, and once I did, they became part of me.

MS for many can be very debilitating, and everyone has different symptoms. Mobility isn't necessarily an issue for me. I have visual, stability and fatigue issues. I get numb, but I haven't had issues where I can't walk. I'm also very sensitive to sunlight;

By Erin Albert

PERSONALLY, it is difficult for me to work on home projects outside in the yard; PROFESSIONALLY, I surround myself with staff, contractors, and a great network of people who support me and assist me with my business. Lastly, I don't dwell on my disease—I can have other people dwell on it for me (doctors, medical practitioners, etc.).

These days, I feel *blessed* to have MS because I see it as my balance. It is the one thing that slows me down. I'm normally a go go go kind of gal, and if God says I need to rest, MS will kick in and make me rest. It is the one thing that slows me down, and reminds me I'm not in charge of everything that happens in life ... so, I'm thankful in that regard that MS gives me that balance.

Obtaining reasonable healthcare for employees as a business owner has to be a huge challenge.

It has been a challenge. My company isn't big enough yet for a group policy, so Phelco has individual policies for employees who need them. Some are on spousal insurance. I personally have an individual policy.

When I started my company, I luckily had COBRA. Then I went directly into an individual policy and didn't have MS at the time, so I didn't have to be interrupted with finding health insurance with a diagnosis of MS. But as a business owner, health insurance for my employees is one of my biggest expenses.

What thoughts have you given to succession planning and business impact preparedness?

Every day I think about the impact of my medical condition on my ability to be productive. Living with MS is unpredictable and uncertain. As a business owner who is single, there isn't anyone who can fill in for me or "handle business" at home, so I have to appropriately position my business to operate the same way. Phelco will continue to exist ONLY if I maintain tools to replace me and my business knowledge/intelligence when that time comes. (Not death, necessarily, but ANY given interruption or emergency.) This is a LEVEL ONE responsibility for Phelco's operability strategy, and it is NOT to be compromised. I place a significant amount of value on our ability to BE THERE for our clients.

Karen
Polis

Follow Mantis[SM] *Money Coaching*

"To 'follow Mantis' means to put that core aspect of yourself, a foundation of spirit, at the helm and let it direct your intellect and ultimately your life."—Joanne Lauck

aren Polis received a double major from Emory University in psychology and art history, and has been a "self-study" in money since her sophomore year. She has worked as a graphic artist and a home organizer, and brings a blend of creativity and organization to her practice. Karen is a Money Coach, certified through the Financial Recovery[SM] *Institute in California.*

Karen and **Follow Mantis**[SM] **Money Coaching** *are committed to helping clients live an authentic and fulfilling life. They help clients get out of the "money fog," develop concrete money skills, and form a positive relationship to money in order to envision and live the life they truly desire. Because money touches almost every part of a person's life, Karen works with clients from a holistic perspective and* *helps them see money as a form of self-care. Some common money challenges that clients may seek help for are: feeling confused and out-of-control over money, lacking basic money management skills, overspending, chronic debt, under earning, having negative feelings about money or about people with money, being fearful of mismanaging inherited or sudden wealth, and not having anyone to talk to about their money. Karen conducts group classes in the greater Philadelphia area and one-on-one counseling sessions by phone to individuals around the country who are ready to transform their relationship to money. You can find her on the web at: www.followmantis.com.*

Please describe your business in one sentence.

I help people feel more control and less stress over their money.

Why did you start your business, where did the idea or concept come from, and why did you start it during a recession?

It's a long story. I had previously worked as a graphic artist in the pharmaceutical industry for many years and was part of a large lay-off (the industry is still doing that today). I then got a temporary position at another pharmaceutical company with the intention of going back to graphic design. That job had me, literally, clicking a mouse button all day long in a makeshift office, using a computer with an extremely poor ergonomic set-up. Within three weeks, I developed severe repetitive strain injury in both my arms. It was painful to even hold open a paperback book. I had to quit that job with only one week left to go.

What I thought was a minor setback that might take a few weeks to heal, ended up being a life-changing event. Six years later, I am still experiencing symptoms from that injury. Unable to work, I was on worker's compensation for the first 2 years, which ended when I received a settlement. I knew the settlement money would last a certain amount of time, during which I would need to find a new career. Going back to computer work was no longer feasible. I was not disabled enough to qualify for assistance, yet I was not able enough to work in any of the areas I had previously worked. Even low-wage, unskilled jobs were beyond my physical capabilities.

I had to find something financially viable that would support the health of my arms and, most importantly, something that I was passionate about. People around me kept telling me, "You have to do *something*—anything." They made many well-meaning, but misguided suggestions, yet I was keenly aware that my injury was a "blessing in disguise," forcing me to pursue only an authentic path. I spent those 4 years that I was out of work, searching—finding and making use of whatever resources were available to me, reading all kinds of self-help books, and taking a variety of classes in order to figure out what to do with my life. Nobody was able to help me and my quest seemed hopeless.

Towards the end of the 4 years, I took a four-week class based on the book *The Passion Test* by Janet Bray Attwood and Chris Attwood. This book is designed to help people figure out what their top five passions are and to help them achieve those passions. For my number one passion, I wrote that I wanted to figure out what my passion was from a career standpoint, because at that time I still had no earthly idea what I wanted to do, let alone what I was physically able to do. One of the class exercises was to write down specifically what each passion would look like even if I didn't yet know what it specifically was. The idea behind that is the clearer you can be about what you want, the easier it is to attract that into your life.

During the last week of the class, I received a free credit report in the mail, and while I was looking through it, the thought came to me: "I bet I could work for the government doing credit repair on a part-time basis to help me get by until I find what it is I really want to do." I started researching on the internet about credit repair and found the Financial Recovery^{SM} Institute (www.financialrecovery.com). I thought that it would make more sense to talk to a school, rather than a potential employer, about whether I could do that type of work with my injury. (I figured most employers would not be very open to hiring somebody with such limitations.)

Single. Women. Entrepreneurs.

When I spoke to the founder of the institute, Karen McCall, she told me they did not teach credit repair. As she explained to me what they *did* teach, I felt chills run through my body. In that moment, I knew that this would be my next career. When I asked Karen about this type of work in regards to my injury, it turns out that she had also had a repetitive strain injury some years back, and was still able to do her work. Of course, this just further confirmed for me that I was on the right path. I then enrolled in the Financial Recovery[SM] Institute's nine-month certification program and became a certified Financial Recovery[SM] counselor. I opened my business, Follow Mantis[SM] Money Coaching, in January 2009.

As for starting my business during a recession, I didn't choose that. After four frustrating years of searching, I had found my "calling"—it just happened to be during a recession.

The challenge with my business is two-fold. First (and this is not specific to the recession), money coaching is a relatively new field, and most people mistake me for a financial planner. So, before someone can decide if they need my service, I must first educate them on what I really do. Second, during these challenging economic times, a lot of people are realizing that they could use some help with their money, but at the same time, they are reluctant to spend money for that help. Ironically, this is probably a time when they could use the type of help I provide most. Money coaching can help people save tremendous amounts of money, and feel so much more peaceful and in control of their lives, but it's hard for people to see that benefit until they start actually doing the work involved. A lot of people are looking for a quick fix, but money coaching is a process. For people who are willing to make that commitment to themselves, the results are profound.

You describe your business as totally different from financial planning. How is it different?

A financial planner has a specific license that allows them to put people into investments. While I can, and do educate clients on some basic investing concepts, I absolutely cannot legally advise someone on which investments to choose or move their money for them, and I do not sell any investment products.

What I do is help people improve the relationship they have with their money in two ways. One way is that we address the practical, number side of things. We track money in and out, and help people see where they are spending their money. People can't hide from their numbers when they are written right there in front of them. We can certainly discuss investing during sessions—it's a very important part of a person's overall money life—but I don't tell people what to do with their money. I act as a facilitator to help people reach their own unique decisions.

The other way I help people is more about their emotional, psychological, and spiritual relationship with money. Knowing the actual numbers often acts as a catalyst for this deeper work. Talking and journaling helps to unearth a person's history and beliefs around money—what things were like growing up, how their parents felt about money, what the common money sayings were within the household, etc. The process gives people insight into why they might be handling their money in certain ways. Just having that insight may be enough for a person to start adopting healthier money behaviors.

In many ways, my job fills the gap of what we were never taught about money in school or from our parents, as well as providing a regular source of support and accountability.

Do you work with a lot of budding and current entrepreneurs, and if so, do they have different issues about money than others? If so, what are those differences you see in your practice, and how do they get resolved?

Yes, I do work with small business owners and people thinking about starting businesses. The main difference with the current or budding entrepreneur is that there's a lot of fear around whether or not they'll have enough money when there's not necessarily a 'steady' income. The money coaching process helps them to see what they have and what they'll need for the lifestyle they want.

It's also very effective for helping people set aside enough money to sustain themselves during downturns or times of inconsistent income. Sometimes it can save a person from pursuing an avenue that's not going to help them reach a financial goal, or to get out of something that's costing them more than it's worth.

On the flip side, a person may choose to do something that's *not* in their best financial interest, but that is emotionally the right thing for them to do. Whatever a person decides, I always want them to base their decision on knowledge, choice, and truth, never on fear.

What advantages do you think you have as a single woman entrepreneur that a married entrepreneur might not have?

Definitely freedom of my time and my environment. In my household, it's just me and my two cats, and I generally don't need the cats' permission to do anything. I rarely set an alarm clock anymore—I just wake up when I'm done sleeping. I can set up meetings to suit my schedule or change dinnertime at the last minute. Since I don't need to "get away" from anyone, my office is in the main room of my home where I can easily move between email and cooking, and all my other household and computer tasks. I have complete privacy when I'm on the phone with a client. Quiet time is easy to achieve in my home—I just turn off the TV!

What about disadvantages?

I think the biggest disadvantage is not having that built-in support system that people get from being in a good relationship. If they need feedback, a boost, a break, or assistance … there's always somebody there for them, assuming that the person is supportive. That can also go the other way: I know a few women who have a significant other who is not supportive of their business, and those women have to contend with hearing a lot of negative and discouraging comments. But I think for the most part, the relationships are supportive. There can also be a financial disadvantage to being single; not having another person's income to help out or fall back on can be scary and stressful.

By Erin Albert

Do you think business ownership has led you to remain single?

I could blame it on that, but honestly, it's mostly by choice. I'm very comfortable being single, and I'd be concerned that being in a relationship would take away some of the freedom I talked about earlier. I'm not entirely closed to the idea, it's just that it's not currently on my "short list."

What advice would you give another single woman who is thinking about starting a business?

Definitely have some kind of business support system in place. I meet with another woman over the phone once a week, for a "mastermind" group. We brainstorm together, give each other feedback, set goals, and celebrate successes in our businesses. It's impossible to think outside of your own brain, so someone else can be invaluable in offering a fresh perspective. I also meet twice a month for a "Counselor's Club" that is run by the Financial Recovery^{SM} Institute and provides continuing education for its certified counselors.

Another suggestion is to join networking groups and go to those meetings on a regular basis. You don't have to spend a lot of money on this. There are plenty of free or low-cost groups available. Even the ones that have a membership fee often have free events for non-members. Put yourself out there. As a single business owner, it's easy to fall into the trap of holing up in your house on the computer all day long. Even if the computer is where most of your clients come from, you will still want to interact with people face-to-face.

Also, be sure to maintain some balance in your life. Keep doing things that you love, other than your business, such as hobbies. You may have to cut back on how much you do them due to time and/or money constraints, but don't stop doing them. You need balance so you don't burn out.

Interesting, you didn't bring up money in your advice ...?

That is interesting. I guess I was considering my own situation when I answered that question. I use the same money-tracking system that I teach to my clients for my own money, and without that, I would be unbelievably stressed. During my years in the corporate world, I was able to save and invest a lot of money. Using this money-tracking system allows me to see just how long that money will last. Because of that, I am now able to build my business without the stress of an additional job. That's a wonderful thing in and of itself, but in my case, it's also a necessity because I would not physically be able to work an additional job. Having a history of healthy money behaviors has given me a tremendous amount of freedom and flexibility in my current endeavors. Now, I get to help others feel empowered around their money.

To answer the original question, people's relationship with money is such an individual thing. Some people need to have a lot saved up in order to feel comfortable starting a business, while others may actually be motivated by stress and have a better chance of success if they have nothing to fall back on.

What about being a single WOMAN business owner? Do you or have you perceived advantages and/or disadvantages to being a woman business owner?

It actually seems somewhat easier to me to be a woman business owner because I think women network and collaborate very naturally. I feel we are not as competitive as men are, and are more genuinely interested in what each other is doing. I perceive these as advantages. There are also many networking groups and other types of business-assistance programs that are specific to women. As for disadvantages, I have not experienced any, probably because I have not expected any. I was raised to believe that men and women are equal in terms of achievement potential. The idea that a woman might be at a disadvantage in the business world seems outdated to me.

What was the best training you received to prepare you as a business owner?

Believe it or not, the best training I received was my arm injury. When I was originally laid off from my graphic design job, I went through a job-transition program the company offered through my severance package (polishing my resume, how to interview, etc.). The package also included an optional two-month self-employment program of which I took advantage. (At the time, I thought I might try going freelance with graphic design or start a business as a professional organizer.)

It was a wonderful program and I learned a lot; however, I was overwhelmed by everything I was learning. Starting a business would require me to obtain a license, register my name, secure a URL, advertise in two specific papers ... and that was just to get started! It all felt like too much to me, and I ended up crawling back into the safety of the corporate world and into that fateful temporary position; not so safe after all.

After being injured, all of that self-employment stuff didn't seem so scary anymore. That's why I say my injury was the best lesson for me on becoming an entrepreneur. It, literally, forced me onto the right path. Not being able to take on temporary or part-time positions, or go back to working at jobs I was currently qualified for, assured that I would not settle for just anything. The injury also required me to prioritize my areas of focus. I only had a limited amount of "arm energy" to use each day, so I had to be judicious in what I chose to do.

Activities like playing video games and meaninglessly surfing the web fell out of my repertoire entirely. I'm much more focused on my priorities now. I'm not saying that I *never* engage in time-wasters anymore, but I do a lot less of that than I used to, and I'm now very aware when I am doing that. My injury also created a "forced balance" to my life. I was no longer able to be on the computer for long stretches of time. Eight-hour days were out of the question. A half-hour at a time was more my speed, interspersed with body-balancing activities such as stretching and walking. (Now I know that every person should be taking short breaks from the computer every 20 minutes or so. Our bodies were not designed to do any single activity for such long periods of time as we ask of them in our modern world.) So I say that my injury was my greatest teacher, because whatever next career I went into, I knew I had to do it my way, at my pace, and love it enough to keep at it.

So, you've always had your business as a full-time venture, correct?

Yes. I started full-time right from the get-go in terms of how many hours I put into my business. The difference is that those hours aren't necessarily from 9 to 5. They are whenever I'm most inspired and energized to work, which ends up being much more effective and efficient for me—not to mention, much kinder on my arms. One of the best things about being my own boss is that I can spread my work out any way I want. In between client sessions, which I conduct over the phone while at my computer, I can choose to get up and do something non-computer-related for a bit, then come back to the computer … sometimes not until 10 p.m. at night. Because I make the rules, I can manage and monitor my arm health and adjust my activities accordingly. I would not be able to do that working at a traditional corporate job.

Did you take on a partner in your business at any time?

Not in the way that I think you're asking. As a coach/counselor, I mostly work one-on-one with clients, so it really doesn't make sense for me to have a partner. But, I have collaborated with some wonderful people on business ventures such as workshops and seminars, and I look forward to doing more of that in the future. Co-hosting events with other business owners has been fun and motivating and helps to get the word out about our collective services to a broader audience.

If you had to start another business, what have you learned that you might do differently—either about yourself, or about how to run a business in general?

I think that the big thing I learned (even before I started this business) is that most of the time, good enough is good enough. If you wait for something to be perfect, it's never going to happen.

By Erin Albert

Having been a "perfectionist" my entire life, I really struggled with this concept. In the past, I researched things to death ("paralysis by analysis"). Now, I try to take action when an idea first comes to me. For example, if I want to create a new class, first I'll get a firm date on the calendar and start advertising. *Then* I'll work on the material for the class. In the past, I would have tried to perfect the material first, so I probably would never have gotten around to actually running the class. I've learned that the class is *never* going to be perfect, especially the first time I run it, but I don't let that stop me.

Also, when I first started this business, I really got caught up in the myriad of resources out there. There are so many people putting things out for various areas of business development and/or self-growth: free newsletters, teleseminars, eBooks, etc. It took a while for me to realize that, while the information may be good, it's coming at a rate much faster than I can process. My email was getting clogged up, I had mounds of eBooks that I never even opened; it was ridiculous. All of those potentially wonderful resources had turned into clutter. I became more discerning about what material I downloaded or signed up for—even if it *was* free. So, if I started something new tomorrow, I'd definitely watch out for information overload.

How important were mentors in your entrepreneurial career?

Extremely important. I have two mentors, both from the Financial Recovery[SM] Institute. While I was in training, my mentor was Karen McCall, the founder of the school. My most memorable mentor session with Karen helped me to choose my business name. That was a big "A-ha!" moment for both of us.

Once I was certified, I started working with another one of the teachers from my school as a mentor. She uses her background studies in the field of human potential to coach her clients, and that is in line with how I want to work with my clients, so I feel like we "get" each other. When I need help with anything at all to do with my business, I can call her for an appointment. She has already walked the same road I'm now on, so her input is invaluable.

Single. Women. Entrepreneurs.

Did you start your business with your own capital?

Most of the capital I've used to start and grow my business has been my own from my years of saving and investing. My parents also help me out with certain things, and they initially paid for me to get my certification. I'm very fortunate to have supportive parents. As a single person, their support becomes even more important since I do not have a spouse's income to rely on.

How important are your social and personal networks to the success of your business?

If you are referring to social networking in order to drive business, it's very important in this field, especially face-to-face contact. That's how people start to recognize me and how I build trust with people. A lot of people are uncomfortable talking about their money, so it really helps if I'm not a stranger to them. Doing presentations, workshops, and classes are all an integral part of how I market myself.

As for my purely personal, non-business networks, while I do not take friends and family on as clients, it's still helpful for them to understand what I do because they might know someone to refer to me or know of useful business resources to share.

What is your personal definition of success, and have you achieved it?

Success for me is a lot about freedom and authenticity and being able to live my life the way I want to live it. The ability to achieve my goals easily, relatively stress-free, and with joy is a good personal definition. Have I achieved it? Portions and degrees of it, I have achieved. I already have a lot of freedom in terms of scheduling my time, and right from the start, I built my business with my value of authenticity at the forefront. Financial success is also important to me, and that is a goal I'm still working on: to surpass my income needs so I can start saving and investing again, which is an area I'm passionate about—a passion I love to instill in my clients so they too can achieve whatever their own definition is of success.

By Erin Albert

Anything else you want to share?

One demographic group that I'm really excited to work with is people in their 20s and 30s—those who are in the beginning or early stages of their financial lives in the working world. There is such a huge potential for this group to achieve financial freedom and the earlier they start working on it, the easier it will be. Unfortunately, an astonishing 95% of our population does not achieve this because they either never learned how, or they didn't act on what they learned. I want to be a catalyst to get people off to the right start and help them see what's possible. It's easy for me to envision a person's financial success—the challenge is getting them to envision this for themselves.

Denise Praul

Accurate Tax Management Corporation

Denise Praul *is the mother of three adult children, Julie, Mark and Jason. She is the grandmother to Nikki and a yet unnamed little one on the way. Denise is a board member for Coburn Place, a not for profit organization that provides education, support, therapy and transitional housing for women and their children who are victims of abusive situations in the Indianapolis, Indiana area. Her passion is to mentor and nurture other female small business owners. She enjoys all types of music, and she loves to dance!*

Accurate Tax Management Corporation *is a property tax consulting company that works with commercial property owners to reduce their real estate tax liability. They accomplish this by reviewing assessed values, filing appeals, attending hearings and negotiating lower assessed values on the taxpayers' behalf. They work throughout the state of Indiana assisting the owners of commercial properties. Their best days are when they can deliver a refund of over paid taxes to one of their clients. You can find* *them on the web at: www.accuratetaxmgmt.com, and on Twitter (@accuratetaxmgmt).*

Can you describe your business in one sentence?
We take the pain out of property taxes.

Love that description! Why did you start Accurate Tax Management?
I was at a turning point in my life and career. My youngest had just turned 18, and I was turning 40. I was looking for a change and more control over my life. I was already working in the property tax consulting industry, so starting Accurate Tax Management Corp. seemed like a good next step. That was 13 years ago, and I haven't looked back.

What advantages do you think you have as a solo business owner that married people don't have?
I think there are a couple of things: first, the decisions we make don't effect a spouse or significant other in our personal lives; that gives us a little more freedom to make potentially risky decisions. Second, I think scheduling is an advantage; I can work the hours I need to or want to, and I don't directly change someone else's life or schedule.

What about disadvantages?
There's no financial fallback, and there's no emotional support directly from a spouse or a significant other. That is hard when you go home and you've had a hard day, or you're trying to make a big decision about your business.

How do you manage around those challenges?
Financially, I try to keep a cushion in the bank for emergencies. For emotional support, I have a really great system of friends and family around me who help keep me grounded.

By Erin Albert

Do you think business ownership has led you to remain single?

I do think that it has led me to remain single. I enjoy the independence of being a business owner, and I like not having anyone to answer to on a regular basis. Because the business does well, I am able to comfortably support myself, which has led me to remain single.

What advice would you give another single woman who is thinking about starting a business?

First, have a cushion of money, at least six months, in the bank. Second, I think women should feel free to do their own thing. Women should take their own personalities, characteristics, and traits and feel free to convey those personalities, characteristics and traits through their businesses, rather than fit into a mold.

What about being a single WOMAN business owner? Have you perceived advantages and disadvantages to being a woman business owner?

I think there are both advantages and disadvantages. The advantage is that women are pretty good at juggling balls, many balls and keeping them all in the air at the same time. That is something I find that I need to do a lot as a business owner. I think another advantage is that women are good at relationships. Relationships come naturally for us and I think that's helpful. There are disadvantages as well. Unfortunately, there are still men in this world who will not deal with women in business. I went on a sales appointment in the past with a male sales representative working for me, and the man we made a call on would only speak to the male salesperson, not me. Men from other countries in our world also have an aversion to doing business with women as well, due to the culture they come from.

We are getting much closer, however, to having equality. I have found during the course of running my business, there has been a strong shift to more female decision makers. My best clients are female decision makers, and we've created our own "buddy system," which has evolved during the course of our business.

Single. Women. Entrepreneurs.

I'm also a member of IndyCREW (The Indianapolis Chapter of Commercial Real Estate Women: www.indycrew.org), which has been a great support and resource for me. The commercial real estate world is a very tough world for women. It is still mostly male dominated. It's nice to have that group of women who are collaborating and helping each other move forward and understand the challenges in the industry. I'm also the only woman owned tax representative firm in the state of Indiana; it's all men except for me. However, it is important for me to state that there are men who completely support women business owners too.

In terms of surrounding yourself with women in business, it is a good idea. However, what I'm cautious about are women who consider the "us vs. them" mentality between women and men in business. It doesn't have to be "us vs. them." That's one of my big pet peeves. We don't have to be anti-men. We can be pro-all and inclusive.

What was the best training you received to prepare you as a business owner?

I think two things had a great influence on me as a business owner: 1. My father—he always instilled hard work and the 'do whatever it takes' mentality. When he was laid off, he has started a small lawn care business or delivered newspapers or pizzas. He was always working and creating income for our family, which was a strong influence upon me. 2. A former employer taught me how to have confidence in my decision making and how to be a good business owner and still be generous and considerate to one's clients and employees. I learned a lot from him.

While I don't have a college degree (I was married with my first child at age 17), I've learned as I go as a business owner. I have taken a lot of great business classes and read many informative books over my career. I've also learned much from others such as CJ McClanahan, Hazel Walker, Tony Robbins, and even Jack Canfield. I'm constantly learning and growing as a business owner and a person. You HAVE to constantly keep learning; if you're not learning in the times we live in, you're going backwards.

By Erin Albert

Did you, or are you running your business as a part-time or full-time venture?

I have always been full-time.

Did you take on a partner in your business at any time?

I actually started this business with a woman business partner who was also my best friend, and it was a stressful and disappointing experience. We had different visions for the business and our work ethics did not match. It didn't work well, so I bought her out of the business several years ago. In the future, I would not take on another partner. However, I will say that I take full responsibility for the disconnect. We should have had conversations up front about the business and our expectations, but you don't know what you don't know. It should have been in writing prior to the start of the partnership, and unfortunately it just didn't work well.

If you had to start another business, what have you learned that you might do differently—either about yourself, or about how to run a business in general?

I think I would get in the game a little more quickly. You can't run a business sitting behind your desk. It took me a while to get out into the world and really create relationships with people, and develop my own reputation and brand with the company. Get out into the world and start meeting people. Even if you don't always do things right, keep on going and learning. ALWAYS continue to learn and grow, whether it is in the realm of technology, creating systems, dealing with employees, or just your own personal growth. Finally, it is really important to be able to embrace change. It happens whether or not you want it to, and if you are slow adapting to that change, you're going to be left behind.

Did you start your business with your own capital?

I'm completely self-funded. I've considered at times getting capital from others, but I don't like owing others. I want to operate the business within its own means. I don't want to overstretch.

Single. Women. Entrepreneurs.

How important are your social and personal networks to the success of your business?

This for me is a hard question. I really view my networks differently. I have a strong business network, but I wouldn't put my business network in my personal network. I really keep the two of them separate. Sometimes that's the way I keep my sanity. I can't talk about the business all of the time. There has to be a place where the business stops and you start as a person. When I started the business, my personal network really wasn't supportive or nonsupportive of the business. I announced I was starting the business at dinner with my family, and my mom looked at me and said, "That's nice, dear," and went back to eating. But from the beginning they weren't a big support factor either way. However, it has worked very well for me.

Why do you think more single/divorced and widowed women start more businesses than men in their respective categories, and does your theory match your own rationale for starting a business?

In my personal opinion, I think a lot of men start businesses for ego reasons—"I own my own business, my name is on the door, and no one can tell me what to do," for example. Women start more businesses from a personal growth perspective, and also for a desire to have more control over their lives. I also think women are very good at watching things grow up and are really good at nurturing. For me, my business is like a child. I think I convey my maternal instincts to this business in many ways. Many women treat their business like their babies, but I don't think men do.

What is your personal definition of success, and have you achieved it?

My personal definition of success is harmony. It is the right mix of family, work, friends, personal time, and sometimes it will be more in one category than another. I never label it as balance, either, because it will never really be fully balanced. I just strive for harmony.

Have I achieved it? No. I think I still have too much business in my whole life. I really put in a lot of time, focus, and thought into the business. If married, that would be different, but because I'm not, I spend a lot of time on the business.

Julia M. Rhodes

KleenSlate Concepts

Julia **M. Rhodes** *is President and Founder of* **KleenSlate Concepts**, *a successful international product development company she founded in 2001. A teacher, Julia developed the solution to a common problem as a teacher: the missing white board eraser. Julia invented, patented, manufactured, marketed and distributed her first product: The KleenSlate® Attachable Eraser for Dry-Erase Markers. Her company now provides creative and novel dry erase products for all aspects of the education market. She single handedly landed contracts with both Office Depot and Staples and understands what it takes to "do business with the big boys." In the past 9 years, she has built a thriving company with a growing line of award-winning dry-erase products and services. Recently, the U.S. Small Business Administration (SBA) Fresno District Office announced Julia had been selected as the 2010 Central California Small Business Person of the Year. She also published a book:* The Right Sisters: Women Inventors Tell Their Stories *which is available at Amazon.com or her website, www.kleenslate.com.*

Single. Women. Entrepreneurs.

As a solo woman business owner, what advantages do you think you have over a married woman business owner?

No one to take care of or ask if it is "OK" on a daily basis is my biggest advantage. Hence, I am able to work into the night and do whatever I want.

What about disadvantages?

My support system is my family and friends, but when it comes to business, having to go it alone day after day is the tough part.

Do you think business ownership has led you to remain single?

No. If anything, I have met more men and seem to be more open to a relationship than I was when I was a teacher.

Why do you think that is?

I am more self-confident about what I can do. I meet more interesting people because I am out of the classroom and in the real world. I travel more and am more engaged with other business owners and run with a different crowd.

Do you agree with the notion that entrepreneurs attract other entrepreneurs? Did or do you?

Yes. I agree that entrepreneurs attract other entrepreneurs. It is a given that we want to share our stories—glean help, brainstorm and even do business with other entrepreneurs. When you share so much, it is easier to want to do that with someone on a daily basis. Entrepreneurs are not easy because their business takes most of their time. So, to find another entrepreneur that is consumed with his/her business allows you to find camaraderie of sorts. He or she understands and supports your lifestyle.

What advice would you give another single woman who is thinking about starting a business?

Join other woman's organizations, network, get out there and shout to the world about your business. Ask questions, share successes, challenges and resources. You can't do it all by yourself. Surround yourself with great people, and find team members that compliment your skills, vision and style. Ask a lot of questions and find the right people to talk to. Get a mentor, a business coach, and join women's organizations like the National Association for Women Business Owners (NAWBO), the Women's Business Enterprise National Council (WBENC), as well as take classes at your local economic development center.

What about being a single WOMAN business owner? Do you think it is easier, the same, or harder than being a single man starting a business?

All I can speak to is being a woman business owner. It is harder to get funding, raise capital, and to be taken seriously as a woman. In one meeting I went to, they asked where the "guy" was they could talk to. So the next time we met, I put a guy's face on a paddle and asked him questions. It was funny, but a true fact, in that they were just not used to seeing women in the role of decision maker or patent holder—at least for my industry, which is office supplies.

What was the best training you received to prepare you as a business owner?

Pure experience was my best training—making mistakes, asking questions, taking the journey. However, I did take classes at the local economic development center and Small Business Development Council (the SBDC). I did get mentors and a business coach when I first started, as I knew virtually nothing about business.

How did the business coach help you?

I have had several—different coaches for different stages of the business. My business coaches helped me with the step-by-step process of setting up and running a business, even simple things, like the acronyms and language. We role-played on how to talk with corporate executives and industry related folks. We created marketing material and public relation pieces. I had life coaches mixed in with business coaches, each one adding value where needed. I also joined Big Fish Nation—which is an amazing year long, life altering coaching program that integrated everything together— the importance of having a vision, setting goals and becoming an expert in your field and in the world. I also grew my business while balancing my life, and I learned the value of balancing my business life with my personal life.

Did you, or are you running your business as a part-time or full-time venture? Why?

At first, I was part-time, as I also was teaching middle school. Soon, it was evident that I needed to choose, and I went with cashing in my retirement and refinancing my house in order to leap into the business world.

Did you take on a partner in your business at any time?

I have been the only working member. I did sell shares early on to get money needed to go to market, make molds, and buy inventory. Today I am in process of buying back my shares from my friends and family that stepped up at the beginning, and I'm now looking for a working partner with money and expertise who can help me take on the world!

If you had to start another business, what have you learned that you might do differently—either about yourself, or about how to run a business in general?

I learned it is not as easy as it seems at first. Make sure you have enough money and good credit and people that know the ins and outs of operating a business around you. Have your accountant, lawyer and banker all working together. Hire the right people, surround yourself with experts in the field, attend more business classes, and don't be afraid to bring in working partners.

How important were mentors in your entrepreneurial career?

HUGE! I could not have crossed the street without getting hit by cars if it had not been for my mentors. For example, when I went to Office Depot to sell my products, I met Shari Francis and AnneMarie Richards. I was naïve and inexperienced in doing business with corporate America. They took me under their wings—yes they are angels—and taught me the "how-tos" of doing business with the "big boys." I also had Lorin Beller-Blake, founder of Big Fish Nation, and my Big Fish community, who showed me the value of networking and building relationships, while taking care of my business and myself. I have Wendy Steele, owner of TapeWrangler, and Rebecca Cohen, founder of RebeccaPlants—amazing entrepreneurs with insight, vision and go-giver attitudes. We make sure to connect on a regular basis and have started working together on various projects!

Beyond mentors, what is your support structure and system? How do you stay motivated as a business owner?

I have a gal in my office, Shelly Kiriluk, and without her, I wouldn't be here today. She holds down the fort when I'm gone making sales calls, going to shows and meeting with customers. She's handling the organization as director of operations. It is critical to have good people internally working with you in your business.

Also, my support system has recently changed in terms of a 'significant other' relationship. After being single for 28 years, I recently found a significant other in my life, and he too is an entrepreneur. He actually was one of my mentors through the evolution of my business, and loaned me the HR person from his company to grow my own business. He also has shown me the power of understanding the numbers. My weakest point in business acumen was financing and numbers. Now, having this support system to bounce ideas around with is amazing.

It is interesting, because prior to meeting him, I just didn't care about a relationship. I had no time. I think when a single entrepreneur gets involved in a relationship, it changes how you run your business, because you find yourself no longer running the business 24/7. You actually take time to eat a decent dinner with a significant other.

Also, it is key to have people in your life who share your vision and keep it real. They don't mind if you're breaking the rules. You have to be very creative about how you do business as a single woman entrepreneur. Ideas are a dime a dozen; it is the action behind them that takes the entrepreneur to the next level. True entrepreneurs aren't afraid to take risks and put it all on the line, because if they don't believe in themselves and their ideas, who else will stand up for them and say, "I believe in you"?

How important are your social and personal networks to the success of your business?

Critical!!! It is not about the product or service as much as it is about the relationships. It is who you know these days, not what you know. Diane McClelland, president of ASTRA, (which is a regional partner of WBENC) showed me the value of networking with Women in Business and the WBENC certification in order to work with corporate America.

Why do you think more single/divorced and widowed women start more businesses than men in their respective categories, and does your theory match your own rationale for starting a business?

I think it is because you don't have anyone saying "no" all the time. You don't hear, "No, we can't afford that," or, "No, I want you home taking care of the kids," or just plain "No." I think women are finding how exciting and rewarding it is to be their own boss, despite the challenges. It fits my own rationale. When you take on the challenge of starting a business and find out you can do it, there is a sense of self-worth. It is so much better than sitting around doing nothing and watching your life go by. It is about participating in a vision—your own vision—and making it a reality. We are only limited by our own imaginations.

What is your personal definition of success, and have you achieved it?

For me, being successful equates to living an easeful, peaceful, useful life. It is about balance in the day-to-day, having time to enjoy the family. I feel I have achieved it in that sense. It is not so much about how much money—yet that is important—but it is about knowing I am making a difference in the world today and having time to enjoy it. That is my definition of success.

What other single women business owners do you admire, and why?

It is not who or how many you know, but it is a quality they possess; their perseverance, positive attitudes, a belief and passion for what they are doing that is so admirable to me. They go the extra mile and do what they do because they know that they can. They find ways to get things done and it doesn't stop with them. These women, and I think most women, have a go-giver attitude, a philanthropic desire to give back, and they do what they do to make the world a better place.

Is there anything else left out that you wanted to add?

The money comes, but the relationships are really the value at the end of the day relative to success for a business owner. It is the difference in the world that the entrepreneur is making that actually motivates the entrepreneur, not just the money. My son Joe, just out of college, is now following in my footsteps. He grew up watching me take risks, leave a stable day job, start a company, and then grow with it. He helped glue felt into erasers in the living room and cheered when the products and company won awards, got the thumbs up from *The Jay Leno Show*, and he videotaped the segment shown on *The Big Idea* show. Joe continues to stay engaged and inspired with KleenSlate. Because he sees what I have done, he knows he can do anything. He still plans on becoming an entrepreneur in the future, but for now he is still taking notes and lending a hand when needed.

Lisa T. Richardson

ATS Professional Learning Center

Lisa T. Richardson *is a Ph.D. candidate in higher education administration, with a primary focus on instructional technology and the accessibility of online learning for students with disabilities. She has a 14-year background in adult and higher education, as well as professional and career development. A single mom and entrepreneur, Lisa balances raising two young boys with the management and growth of her other baby, the* **ATS Professional Learning Center.**

The ATS Professional Learning Center teaches hands-on technology courses for educators, entrepreneurs, and other public and private sector leaders. From social media to SMART Boards, webquests to accessible web design, online courses to marketing on a nonexistent budget, they focus on providing practical do-it-now learning opportunities that improve customer and community relations, process improvement, and knowledge-sharing in organizations. Located just outside Atlanta in Marietta, GA, you can reach them at (770) 726-9960, online at www.ATSLearn.com, or on Twitter: @ATS_Atlanta.

Single. Women. Entrepreneurs.

Please describe your business in one sentence.

ATS Professional Learning Center offers technology courses for people who hate technology.

Why did you start ATS?

I had been working with adult students as an academic advisor. They had a lot of problems and challenges with digital literacy. They were struggling, but I saw how they could overcome their technological challenges to make their lives better, doing research online, etc., and found myself coaching them through this process. When I went to graduate school, I started helping faculty with technology too. When I was close to graduation, I figured out that I really liked helping adults learn technology. I enjoyed helping others through technology, so I started ATS in 2008.

What advantages do you think you have as a single woman business owner that married people don't have?

Well, having a 9 year old and a 21 month old presents extra challenges being a single mom. However, my biggest advantage is that I don't have to report to someone else. If I need to stay late at work, the sitter can stay late with the kids, and I don't have to justify to a significant other staying late at work (my office is outside my home). If I'm working from home, the children are already in bed. There is no other person competing for my attention.

What about disadvantages?

I don't have anyone to decompress with at the end of my day. I'm still a one-woman operation, but I do have instructors who help. I do all the risk analysis, strategy and business development for my company, and I also do all the heavy lifting at home. I have to do it all by myself. I have family support, but primarily, it's me.

Do you think business ownership has led you to remain single?

I wouldn't say so necessarily. I know that I don't socialize very much because I don't have time. When I go to networking events,

By Erin Albert

I'm networking from a business standpoint; I'm not looking for a date. I'm just not thinking about dating.

What advice would you give another single woman who is thinking about starting a business?

Find other friends who are suffering like you are. Because I'm a single mom and not running a home-based business, it's a challenge for me to talk to other women in business in general. Other women in the networking organizations I belong to have husbands and help at home. At times, I do feel a bit isolated. Find other single women in business in your area with whom you can commiserate. Also, find people who are not always upset with the world, either. I'm blessed to be doing what I want to do and don't have to worry where the next dollar is coming from for my family. I see the struggle, but I also see the benefits of being on my own.

Do you perceive advantages and disadvantages to being a WOMAN business owner?

I think my clients might relate to me better as a woman in the industry I'm working in—technology education. My style is to guide my clients through their technology education experience. If I was a male, some of my customers might think I was less of an educator, because some men in IT talk in coder language, for example, and do not speak on a level that people can understand. The major disadvantage in technology as a woman business owner is the expectation that I may not know what I'm talking about because I'm a woman in IT, and because I look young.

What was the best training you received to prepare you as a business owner?

My parents gave me the best gift to prepare me, which was education for education's sake. I wasn't worried that I had to find a job at the end of college. I started out in college as pre-med and didn't like the site of blood, so then I found education. I loved education, but I really didn't enjoy teaching children. It took me some time to explore and find my niche. It was really adult education that I loved. That niche led me to start my business, which allowed me to use my strengths.

Did you, or are you running your business as a part-time or full-time venture? Why?

Full-time. It's always been full-time for me. I had my younger son while working at another organization and went to the hospital early. I didn't have FMLA where I was working and was released from that position when I went into the hospital. What I intended to have as a part-time operation turned into a full-time operation when I was on my feet again.

Did you take on a partner in your business?

(Laughing) I'm laughing because I was supposed to have a partner who was a former client in this business. Because nothing was ever written down, I should have known better, for whatever reasons—being unwilling or unable to fulfill his part of the bargain, etc., I didn't take on a partner. I could tell he didn't know what I did or how I did it, but it was partially my fault the partnership didn't work. At that point, bootstrapping REALLY became bootstrapping! I don't think I'll be seeking a partner or even an investor in the near future.

If you had to start another business, what have you learned that you might do differently—either about yourself, or about how to run a business in general?

I might try something that requires that I wear fewer hats. I love what I do, but I realize that I kind of set myself up in this current business so that I HAVE to do everything, and it may be easier next time around to search for someone who is like minded and understands the mission and can carry some of the load. That way I don't have to have a stranglehold on every single thing. Ironically, I am looking at the next venture today. This will be a fun one! My current business is serious, so the next one I want to be fun.

By Erin Albert

How important were mentors in your entrepreneurial career?

Because I'm kind of a loner, I didn't pursue mentorship as well as I could have. I do have a group of peers. We commiserate, share, and actually mentor each other. We're hitting the bumps together, trading war stories, and sharing best practices. This group naturally formed from a very strong and small group of core girlfriends, who are like-minded: single, driven, and entrepreneurial. One is a best friend from high school, and we really have grown into the natural order of being friends and now we are business buddies too.

Did you start your business with your own capital?

My own capital. Bootstrapping from day one. My parents are investing in the business. They're probably the only people I would trust at this point.

Why do you think more single/divorced and widowed women start more businesses than men in their respective categories, and does your theory match your own rationale for starting a business?

I think single women like their independence and have a strong desire to be successful. Many of them don't like to be beholden to a company or another organization for them to pursue their own ventures. They seek ideas and grow businesses that are personal to them—and that meet their own personal values, vision and mission.

That definitely reflects my own reasons for starting ATS. I feel that people should not feel trapped in their lives. In my world of digital literacy, a person not knowing what they don't know keeps them from reaching success in business and education. People need the ability to apply critical thinking and research skills to advance and not be held to just having "any" job. One of my girlfriends says, "If you're looking for ANYTHING, you'll find NOTHING." I believe that. There will be sacrifices along the way to get what it is that you truly want.

I'm good at quitting jobs too. I worked for several colleges and universities and decided to go out on my own. One thing my friends always laughed at me and joked about was that I couldn't stand to not be happy at work. Once I decided there was no longer any further advancement for me at an employer, I'd jump ship and go to another place. Although some might think that would be a bad reflection on my resume, in retrospect I now think each and all of those experiences helped me to run my business exactly the way I want to today.

What is your personal definition of success, and have you achieved it?

My personal definition of success is being able to feel secure in that I'm doing what I want to do. That I'm providing an important service. I'm able to go home at night and see that my kids are well taken care of. Being able to sleep at night knowing that I've been a blessing to others and that I'm loved. I would say yes, I feel successful. I'm happy with my life and content. Life is good!

Anything else as a single woman entrepreneur?

Make sure that you're happy doing what you're doing, because you'll be doing a lot of it! For the single part of being an entrepreneur: if your desire is to not be single, don't approach it as a task to be "completed." Rather, in your own contentment and happiness in doing what you're doing, eventually you'll bump into the like-minded person who should be looking for you. It may take awhile but you should be happy doing what you're doing first.

What about being a single woman entrepreneur and mom in the South? What is the business climate like in Atlanta for the woman entrepreneur?

[I have to say that] I'm actually from the Bronx. But yes, there are lots of women's networking organizations in the South. The SCORE center here in the Atlanta area is very good. NAWBO Atlanta has a wide variety of events and educational opportunities. Also, Atlanta NAFE (or the National Association of Female Executives) just restarted. There are also a lot of smaller more industry-oriented organizations too, like StartupChicks (www.startupchicks.net), which is a group of women entrepreneurs mentoring each other with networking and inspiration. I'm also education and professional development chair for Project Single Moms™ (www.projectsinglemoms.com) Atlanta chapter, which I think is a great organization.

What about being a single mom entrepreneur? Can you share more about that and the extra challenges associated with being a single mom?

Supporting the single mother entrepreneur is a passion of mine. Before I discovered Project Single Moms, I wanted to start an organization of single moms myself. I was thinking more of a professional networking group for single moms, and I'm working on that idea, but it would be incredibly time consuming. The challenge of the single mom is that your time is limited. Also in my case, the fathers are not as involved in the lives of my children. One is out of state and the other is in a high-powered position. The lion's share of caring and raising the children is in my lap.

My business also requires a lot of time and effort. My networking time is very limited. Growth of my business really depends upon on gaining exposure for us and it has been a serious challenge for my business. To manage around this, I have a small army of responsible caregivers. I am very close to my former in-laws, and although my ex-husband is now remarried, he is involved in our son's life to the best of his ability, and so are his parents. His dad is here in Atlanta as well. They take care of the boys for me as much as they can.

The best way for me to manage networking is to have a strong grasp of my social media strategy. I definitely have a deep presence online. In Atlanta, the way to do business is face-to-face and relationship-oriented. While I do talk to a lot of people online, I'm actually getting more business out of state than locally because I am online more. People need to see me and come to ATS because they want me to teach them and that also has been a challenge. I'm still

Single. Women. Entrepreneurs.

working on that.

Marcy
Rubin

Certified Professional Life Coach:
Worldwide Services for the Bipolar Disorder Community

Marcy Rubin *is highly respected among the bipolar disorder community for her positive attitude, kindness and unconditional support. Hearing her personal story, living with bipolar disorder, along with professional life coach training, client successes, time spent mentoring, hours educating herself and the constant interaction with the mental health community, you'll understand how her perspective of the illness has transitioned over time. Today, Marcy navigates her place in this process by comfortably stepping into the role as life coach, mentor and friend. Her passion is to remain a positive influence and help break the stigma commonly associated with people diagnosed with bipolar disorder.*

Marcy works with clients all over the world making it possible for everyone in the bipolar disorder community to have an opportunity to get a professional life coaching experience. As a certified life coach, Marcy is trained to unleash passions, inspire, motivate, and help people stay focused. Marcy truly believes anything is possible. She is committed to the life coaching process of encouraging people to set goals, embrace new opportunities and create strategies to achieve a life filled with happiness, balance and value in living. Her clients range from those diagnosed with bipolar disorder, to anyone affected by a life altering illness like bipolar. You can find her coaching site at: www.MarcyRubin.com.

*Marcy knows education is the best way to break stigmas. To help close the gap between the many perspectives of bipolar disorder, she utilized her life coach training and founded **Bipolar United Worldwide**, a unique support system that encourages open, interactive, informational conversation between everyone in the bipolar community. You can locate this organization on the web at: www.BipolarUnitedWorldwide.com.*

Can you describe your business in one sentence?

My life coaching business works with the philosophy that certain areas of one's life may require more focus than others; however, all areas are interconnected and changes in one can positively impact others as well.

Why bipolar disorder? Where did you passion for helping others with this stem from?

In the beginning, I was searching for ways to help myself be better regardless of being diagnosed with bipolar disorder. And, the more I learned, the clearer it became: the stigma around mental illness is so strong that often people don't seek the help they need and deserve. Working with a life coach is an asset for anyone, but finding a coach who understands the unique issues associated with bipolar disorder wasn't that simple. So, I made the decision to be open about my own diagnosis and offer a safe place for others to address their goals with someone who knows what their challenges are like. It's not about the illness, it is how much we let stigma affect our vision of possibilities.

By Erin Albert

What advantages do you think you have as a solo business owner that married people don't have?

An advantage to being a single woman and a business owner is not having the additional stress of balancing the priorities of family and career.

What about disadvantages?

A disadvantage of being a single business owner is work can become the main focus of your life, putting everything else in the backseat. You have to set your own limitations.

Do you think business ownership has led you to remain single?

I apply my life coaching philosophy towards prioritizing and balancing all aspects of my life. To date, being a business owner hasn't affected my relationships.

What advice would you give another single woman who is thinking about starting a business?

Do your research and understand the amount of time it may possibly take to get your business up and running. The process can be demanding. It's important not to become so consumed you neglect to take time out for personal experiences.

Do you think there are advantages/disadvantages to being a single business owner? Do you think it is harder, or easier?

The advantages and disadvantages depend upon the type of work personality you have and what profession you choose. I enjoy socializing with other people. As a career, life coaching gives me the freedom to interact positively with people daily. If you are not self-motivated, going it alone could result in not pushing yourself, resulting in lower accomplishments. Choose a career that matches your lifestyle, values and preferences.

What was the best training you received to prepare you as a business owner?

Past career choices, formal life coach training and interaction within the mental health community all equally influence how I coach. My career choices allowed me the opportunity to interact with many people at all levels and in return gave me first hand knowledge of the diversity in personalities. Professional life coach training taught me how to read between the lines, really hear what is not being said, and also how to empower others to see that anything is possible. Keeping involved in the mental health community is the most important aspect. It doesn't matter what profession you choose, staying updated on what is going on in your industry is key to making a difference.

Did you, or are you running your business as a part-time or full-time venture? Why?

Life coaching typically takes a 3-6 month commitment; therefore, clients come and go on a regular basis. Without continual effort towards networking, the business would quickly fail. Word of mouth is my best recommendation, so it's important for me to actively pursue opportunities that could result in new business.

If you had to start another business, what have you learned that you might do differently—either about yourself, or about how to run a business in general?

Research how successful the average person in that industry is. Also, it is key to find a mentor to help guide you through the process.

How important were mentors in your entrepreneurial career?

In my opinion, having mentors is very important. Anyone who can positively influence you towards reaching your goals is an asset.

By Erin Albert

Did you start your business with your own capital?

I started my business with my own funds. To date, needing additional financing hasn't been an issue. That may change as my career goals change.

How important are your social and personal networks to the success of your business?

Making connections—social or personal—influences my success one hundred percent. I'm an authentic person. My passion to help others see the positive in everything is evident to anyone who knows me. It has been my experience that people are intrigued by the life coaching process and curious to learn more about anything that could bring goals or dreams into reality.

What is your personal definition of success, and have you achieved it?

Success is an ongoing experience of opportunities. Success isn't just the end result; it's about the effort put into achieving your visions.

Becky Ruby

lilly lane, llc

Becky **Ruby** *is an Indianapolis-based, Chicago-raised entrepreneur with a love for all things creative. Following her graduation from Butler University, Becky worked as a fundraiser and event planner in the non-profit industry, where she found herself routinely designing centerpieces for events and enjoying the challenge of creating on a budget. When a friend contacted her for assistance in creating wedding flowers, she readily agreed, and embarked on what would become a dream career. Leaving her 9-5 job in 2009 and never looking back, Becky has found her passion in the art of creating fabulous florals and is absolutely in love with, "the job I never knew I was always meant to do!"*

Becky is a member of the International Special Events Society (ISES) and currently serves on the Board of Directors for ISES Indiana (www.isesindiana.com). Her tips on "How To Start A Flower Shop" have been published on eHow.com at: www.ehow.com/ how_6369234_start-profitable-flower-business.html. In addition to professional groups, Becky is a member of the St. Margaret's Hospital Guild, serves on the Herron-Morton Place Association Board, and volunteers with the Indiana AIDS Fund "Spotlight" fundraiser as a member of their marketing and outreach committee.

Lilly lane *was founded in 2007 by Becky Ruby. Originally a hobby-turned-side-project, lilly lane quickly blossomed (no pun intended!) into a thriving small business. In June of 2009, lilly lane became a full-time endeavour for Becky, who then worked from her historic downtown home. Thanks to the support of many friends and clients, it quickly became apparent that working from home would not be possible, and in April of 2010, lilly lane opened its doors in Midtown Indianapolis. You can find lilly lane online at www.lillylaneflowers.com and www.facebook.com/lillylaneflowers.*

Can you describe your business in one sentence?

We are a special event and special occasion floral design shop.

What advantages do you think you have as a single business owner that married business owners don't have?

Because I am not married and do not have children, there is a certain lack of expectation—not in terms of success, but in terms of the fact that no one is counting on me to have household tasks taken care of. That "lack of expectation" also extends to the fact that I don't have to worry about others relying on me to make my business an instant success. No one but me depends on my income, expects me to have a 401K, or needs me to be saving for college right now. My time is also much more flexible as a result. If I need to work until 11 p.m., I can. If I have to come in the following day at 5 a.m., that's fine too. I can definitely see how the "lack of expectations" I enjoy could put a strain on a marriage.

What about disadvantages?

The advantages of not having a partner or family to depend on me also create the disadvantage: I don't have them to lean on, to create the "safe haven" that married entrepreneurs might enjoy.

I'm on my own. While I am dating someone who is supportive of my endeavors, we are not married, and should I fail, I don't have someone else's income to fall back on.

Do you think business ownership has led you to remain single?

Interestingly, it's just the opposite. When I started my business, I also started dating my boyfriend which happened to be just a few weeks after I left my full-time job. It's nice to have someone who says, "I support you," and he is very understanding about times when I have to say, "No, I can't go out tonight because I have to set up at 5 a.m. for a wedding tomorrow morning." Because he has never known me to have a "traditional job," we've been able to define what a "normal life" means for us from the very beginning. For example, before I started my business, I had jobs with most weekends off— the time you might naturally spend with your boyfriend. Now, I work most Saturdays setting up weddings, and don't mind at all that he goes golfing nearly every Saturday morning! We've figured out, through trial and error, when we can spend time together, and made sure that we do find the time even during the busiest weeks.

How did you start your business?

It honestly started as an accident. I was 24 years old and working in my second fundraising job. In my first, I worked a lot of weekends, but my second job was strictly 8-5, and I got bored! I'd already been making arrangements on the side for work events (after all—with nonprofits, if you can save money on something, you do!) and started to pay attention to what people had to say about them.

Surprised by the very positive feedback, I started becoming more interested in making arrangements and created some for a party at my parents' house—to even more positive feedback, and the first suggestion that I could potentially do this as a career. Later that month, as a New Year's resolution, I asked myself, "Why not?" I was going to turn 25 that year and thought it was an excellent age to start my first company, if I felt like I got a sign to do so.

Single. Women. Entrepreneurs.

Just a few days later, I received a call from a friend. His roommate—another friend—was getting married in July, and the florist had just cancelled. Would I do the flowers? I considered that my sign!

Since that first wedding was in July, I chose it as my "have a business by" date, and I just launched right into it. I designed a logo, picked a company name, and incorporated it. Ironically, I never considered going to another floral shop as an employee. I already had a day job! Soon we were a legal business registered with local wholesalers and I was Googling things I needed to know, like "How do I pay sales tax?" and "Am I wiring this boutonniere correctly?" I was hooked!

I continued to do a few weddings and events on the side, attending a few bridal shows to get more clients, though at this point I was not widely advertising for my services and was obtaining work largely through referral.

When did you start thinking about this as a full-time entrepreneurial gig?

I kept the business part-time for about 18 months (or 1 year from that first wedding). After that, I was getting too busy to take on any more clients and continue to work my day job, but I didn't quite have the client base to generate a paycheck.

It was April 2009, when I started thinking I had to take the business in one of two ways: either keep the business going on the side (and only take on 1-2 weddings per month) and keep my day job, or just go for it and do it full-time. I then decided to talk to an advisor about what it would really take to live on, and my brother moved in with me to share housing costs and help me stretch bill payments.

I quit my job in June 2009, and I gave myself six months with the business. I knew that most couples get engaged between Thanksgiving and Valentine's Day, so I knew I could always go back to a day job if I didn't pick up enough business at the end of the year.

Are your parents entrepreneurs?

Yes, in different ways. My dad is a pathologist, and though he has owned a practice for quite awhile, his practice had been based in a hospital until April of 2009. He took the practice and went out on his own at the same time I started lilly lane full-time. It has been fascinating talking to him and sharing stories, because his business and my business have had similar experiences since our inceptions. What's interesting is that he is working on a very different business and at a very different scale—his business is ten times the size of mine, and he has much more risk and inventory than I do. But, we're both still seeing the same time "trends" over the first 18 months of new business ownership.

My mom never owned a business per se, but in terms of time management and multitasking, she's the role model. I learned from her how to get things done. Some of her more memorable roles include serving as PTA president, teaching English-Second-Language courses at our elementary school and through an adult education program (both things she still does), volunteering with the Girl Scouts, the Boy Scouts, the local retirement home, our animal rescue shelter, a Golden Retriever rescue group ... and so on. My mom is the reason that I considered it perfectly normal in high school to not only attend class all day, but also pass on a study hall so that I could take additional classes, rehearse nearly every day with our theatre department, and hold a part-time job in the evenings and on weekends. Both my parents had a really strong work ethic!

They say entrepreneurs attract other entrepreneurs—did you in terms of your significant other?

Yes and no. He currently works a traditional 8-5 job; however, his field (marketing) is probably one that I would consider more entrepreneurial than most, with many of the same traits making a good entrepreneur also making a good marketer. Other, more traditional workers might not understand my wanting to run my own business, but my boyfriend has many entrepreneurial qualities, and he gets it. We are supportive and proud of each other—we just have to work around the fact that my hours sometimes mean I'm heading in to work at 4 a.m.! Luckily, my business is also unique in terms of planning ahead for time off. Unlike a retail florist, I have a lot of flexibility by not guaranteeing open hours. I can look ahead and block out a weekend off, or a weeklong vacation, and know that it won't be a problem to take that time.

What advice would you give another single woman who is thinking about starting a business?

First of all, do it. Go for it. On a more practical side, learn to manage your time. You're going to love what you do, and that means you're going to work harder than you ever have. You'll wake up at 3 a.m. to work. You'll dream about work. You'll work 20 hours a day. Learn to manage your time, and if you need to, seek someone out to help you do that.

Another practical piece of advice is to set aside money before you get started—whatever you need to have to feel comfortable taking the risk. If you're not working currently, this might be more flexible. If you are working, you should think about giving yourself a deadline (mine was six months). The last thing you want to do is wind up at the bank, begging for a loan or forgiveness on a home foreclosure, and having to explain that you quit your day job without having a plan in place. Finally, don't burn your bridges in your "past life." You might need a reference in the future—or just referrals!

What was the best training you received to prepare you as a business owner?

Honestly, I don't know. I received fantastic training on how to make floral designs through the Chicago School of Floral Design, which was an 8-week commitment, twice a week.

But as far as running the actual business, I just don't know that I ever questioned my ability to do it. I was naïve and said, "Hey, let's do this" and then just went and did it. My dad, and others, have given or recommended to me many books over the years, but I've never been good about reading them. I should probably start, but now I just don't have time!

Advice-wise, outsourcing the "little things" has been the best advice I've received. I have outsourced some things like payroll and accounting, and brought in some part-time assistants to help with smaller tasks that allow me to focus on the big things.

Did you write a business plan?

Yes and no. I had a to-do list in a spiral notebook, and as I shared previously, I had a "deadline date." Now, I operate more from a "tipping point" mentality as I've grown my business. For example, when I was doing too much at home, I then rented a studio. When I couldn't do everything on my own anymore, I hired a contractor. As soon as I was financially viable, I hired a bookkeeper. Setting a plan for this business is not easy. For example, I can figure out what the average cost of a wedding needs to be and how many I need to do to keep my doors open, but I can't make those girls use me, or to spend a specific amount.

I've had to become a lot more flexible—a hard lesson for someone who likes to plan! I usually have a daily schedule but have become used to the fact that I almost never make it through a day without some change to the plan. But then again, having a flower shop was never "the plan!" This business was not a childhood dream. Like many girls, I probably thought at some point that it would be fun to work in a flower shop—but never aspired to start one until about a month before I actually did. Like many people who've started a business, or two, or three, I've probably started about 40 businesses over the years in my head. I'm constantly asking myself, "Wouldn't it be cool if …?" Often, it's not the right time, or it is something that would cost a lot in start-up or require me to invent something about which I have no actual knowledge. This particular business happened to come along at the right time, and I built it with virtually no start-up capital using a skill set I already had.

Did you take on a partner in your business?

I haven't had partners, financial or otherwise, in this business. In the future, I could see a strategic merger with another, as a natural partner business—something that would cover a component we do not currently offer. There are a couple of businesses that already exist in which I could see working with as a larger entity together. However, I don't see taking on an individual partner as we exist now.

I've already been, and am sure I will continue to be, approached by people who want to collaborate. Some of these opportunities make absolute sense, but others, though they may sound like a good opportunity at first, make me question, "What is it about this that isn't right for me?" What I've discovered is that it might be a great idea, but it is not in the direction I'm going, so it's not worth it for me strategically. I've passed on a few opportunities that had great potential, but didn't mesh with my goals.

If you had to start another business, what have you learned from this experience that you might make you do something differently next time?

As a type-A perfectionist, I've had to accept that I'll make mistakes! My best advice to myself or to another businesswoman would probably be don't feel like you have to do everything, or say yes to everything, or even to accept all forms of help when they are offered. Someone may come to you with a fantastic offer, or use of his or her services, or assistance with something. Think about whether you really would have sought that person out if they hadn't come to you, and if you wouldn't have, don't do it!

I learned this lesson early on when I hired a friend-of-a-friend to do something for me, and learned the important lesson when I wound up just having to re-do that project later, at greater expense and additional challenge. If I had been honest with myself, I probably would have looked at this person's portfolio with greater objectivity and said, "No."

How important were mentors in your entrepreneurial career?

Mentors have been extremely important to me. My dad, of course, has been an extremely big influence on me as an entrepreneur, and my mom as the ultimate multitasker. I also work with an executive coach based in Chicago, Dr. Chuck Polcaster. It is fantastic to have an objective third party to discuss the business with and to help me focus on the important things. For example, when I first started the business, our discussions centered on how to set schedules, manage time, and develop client relations. Now we talk about once a month about more long-term planning items.

Did you start your business with your own capital?

Yes. Luckily, I never needed a loan, as I was able to build my business out of my home. I used BizFilings® to incorporate my LLC and a small amount of personal capital for things like branding, logo, and so forth. Inventory was acquired only after I had contracted clients.

How important are your social and personal networks to the success of your business?

Absolutely critical! My network IS my business. I tried a few forms of advertising, and have found that online is best for my business. However, my clients (my network) are a huge source of referrals for me, with about a third of my 2011 wedding business projected to come from girls-who-know-girls whose weddings I did in 2009 or 2010, or who are getting married at venues where I have done weddings.

In addition to our website, lilly lane also maintains a Facebook page to showcase photos and updates, and allow clients to interact with each other. Facebook also allows us to create a "buzz" by posting photos of events happening that day, special offers for our Facebook friends, and so forth.

We do advertise on theknot.com, where we get many of our non-referred wedding clients. I wish that there were similar sites for other aspects of events and home decorating. For example, I love to do holiday home décor, but there's not a certain website that people can go to and search for "home décor in my area" like they can for wedding services.

Single. Women. Entrepreneurs.

What is your personal definition of success, and have you achieved it?

Yes, I think I've achieved success. I am happy with what I'm doing, I'm proud of what I'm doing, and I have a future in what I'm doing. I've achieved a work life balance, which constantly ebbs and flows, and I can pay all my bills! With that definition in mind, I guess I've been successful since the day I knew I'd never have to go back to a day job.

Any other points not asked that you want to share?

One of the things I've been thinking about since being asked to do this interview is why some women succeed, and others don't. Why do solo women thrive at being entrepreneurs and married women don't achieve success as easily? Why are some women able to work for themselves and others aren't? I think it has a lot to do with social patterns, independence, and companionship, and perhaps some of the other women interviewed will have better ideas than I do on this!

Looking at my own situation, I know that part of my success is because I'm an independent person. I choose to be in a relationship with my boyfriend and I love him, but I've also lived on my own and taken care of myself.

Starting a business can be very isolating, especially if you are leaving a social workplace in order to do so. I left a workplace where I had several good friends, and had to work very hard at creating new social experiences for myself since I no longer had daily interactions. Now, I'll bring my dog to work on quieter days when I know I'll be alone in the studio!

And maybe that is part of why solo women (single, widowed, divorced) have success when they start businesses; they've already experienced being able to survive on their own. I can see how being married and/or being very socially tied to your job can be a hindrance in successful entrepreneurship. Simply put, you're probably more reluctant to make yourself more isolated, and less likely to achieve success as a result.

Jennifer Ruby, AICP, JD

Ruby Law

J **ennifer G. Ruby** *is the attorney-owner at Ruby Law. Ruby Law counsels individuals and businesses on estate and succession planning and administration as well as general business issues. Jennifer founded and runs the successful* **Finances 101 for Young Professionals** *seminar series, (www.finances101.us), started in 2005. She is admitted to practice in Indiana and New Mexico. Jennifer earned her B.S. degree from Purdue University, and her M.Pl. and J.D. degrees from Indiana University. She serves as the Secretary of the City of Indianapolis-Marion County Information Technology Board, President of the Warren Township Development Association Board and on the Indiana University— Indianapolis School of Public and Environmental Affairs Alumni Council. Jennifer has been recognized many times over the years; most recently being named one of the Forty under 40 by the* Indianapolis Business Journal *in February 2010. She is also a member of the American Bar Association, Indiana State Bar Association and Indianapolis Bar Association and the applicable business, elder* *law, real property, probate, tax and trust sections. You can reach her through the Ruby Law website—www.ruby-law.com, by email: Jennifer@ruby-law.com, by phone: (317) 332-3757, on Twitter: @ruby_law or on Facebook or LinkedIn.*

Ruby Law counsels individuals and businesses on estate and succession planning and administration as well as general business issues. Ruby Law's environment is customer service, community involvement and family first. Being proactive allows more control over who, what, when, where and how. Ruby Law is an alternative to large firm competition and in-house counsel corporate positions for women attorneys who want to be respected for the knowledge and experience they have while still enjoying community and family involvement.

Can you please describe your business in one sentence?

We help women between ages 45 and 65 get their parents, their families and their businesses in order.

What advantages do you think you have as a solo business owner that married people don't have?

More time and flexibility to manage our lives because we have no spouse to answer to regarding time commitments, financial commitments or allocations of dollars, or other oversight/shared responsibilities. Also, women are born multi-taskers, and owning a business allows us the flexibility to schedule and meet all our commitments.

What about disadvantages?

No safety net—no one to bring in the money if a deal falls through or a bill isn't paid on time. No one obligated to help out emotionally, physically or otherwise.

Do you think business ownership has led you to getting married?

I don't think that it had any effect on my getting married. But, being a business owner and the flexibility that comes along with it allowed me to help deal with my father-in-law's multiple heart attacks in 2005, my mother's thumb, wrist and elbow surgery for carpel tunnel in 2005 and later her broken leg in spring 2006, morning sickness in fall 2006, birth in summer 2007, my husband's illness in spring 2008, and my insomnia and related health issues for 2 years, which were resolved with surgery for a deviated septum in October 2010. Life throws a lot at you sometimes, more the older you get, especially when you are sandwiched between your children and aging parents. Owning your own business can give you the flexibility you need to deal.

You married after starting your business. They say entrepreneurs attract other entrepreneurs. Did you?

Yes and No. My husband is a financial executive by day, but has a part-time vintage guitar instruction, repair and appraisal company. Music is his passion. His business went dormant while we were courting, and his partner abandoned the business. But as of last Christmas, his new web presence is rebuilding his client base. He has my full support.

What advice would you give another single woman who is thinking about starting a business?

The advice I give every person thinking about starting their own business is this: From my personal anecdotal history (at least 3 different ventures), I believe it takes a business 6-9 months before people BELIEVE that you are serious about being in business for yourself and have faith that you will be around long enough to feel confident in hiring you or buying your goods. If you can get a contract with government or a corporation, this may cut down the timeframe, but then you are at the mercy of their payment schedule, which is often a month or more behind. That is why in addition to the capital outlay in setting up your business (which business initiation costs are not tax deductible—continuing costs are), you need to have a way to pay all your bills for at least 6-9 months, and you may not be profitable for 3-5 years.

Single. Women. Entrepreneurs.

So first and foremost, do your homework. Is it a viable business model, are you passionate and determined to make the business work? Will the business cash flow be enough to support your lifestyle and your business needs? Or have you created a 'nest egg' big enough to get you through at least 6-9 months? You can also ask for business loans through the SBA or local bank, but given the banking crisis, that may not be so easy now.

Do you think there are advantages/disadvantages to being a single business owner? Do you think it is harder, or easier?

Honestly, I think there are pros and cons depending on how you look at it. On one hand, I loved being single, getting to do what I wanted, when I wanted, and how I wanted. When you bring another person into that mix, everything narrows to a degree. You have to try to make sure your schedules mesh and there's that wonderful question: "What do you want to do tonight for dinner?" That one question speaks volumes to me about being in a relationship.

From that perspective being single can be easier for running a business. Although my husband supports me in theory and generally to the outside world, at home he is often less than supportive. Far too many discussions have started out about one thing and turned into a fight about my business. I can't count the number of times that he has asked me to quit, close the business, and go to work for another law firm, so we can give up the financial stress and have a regular pay check. That is hard to take when you are building your business and taking care of your daughter full-time. But, I understand where he is coming from … I took on clients that I should NOT have taken on in my first year, who didn't pay me—rookie mistake—and if you don't make mine, you will likely make others. I proudly stated that I had not taken on a new non-paying or slow paying client since Fall of 2005—until this economy. I currently have a few slow-paying business clients.

Spousal emotional support is key because you will be putting your money, heart, sweat and much more than 40 hours a week into the business to make it successful. If your spouse is not behind you, it makes the road to success a lot more difficult—especially on your emotionally down days. Your spouse won't completely understand what you are trying to accomplish or what you are going through unless they have been an entrepreneur themselves—and they still might not know.

On the other hand, I love my husband and my daughter. I can't imagine my life without them. My daughter is the best thing that I ever did, and I highly recommend having children because it's meant more to me than I ever could have imagined. There is a lot to be said about a relationship to keep you grounded and the idea of growing old with someone.

What about being a single WOMAN business owner?
Do you think it is easier, the same, or harder than being a single man starting a business?

We are the best multi-taskers, and we are gaining ground more than ever with the flexibility of the work environment—cell phones, email, Skype, Twitter, etc. I sincerely thank every woman, who before me, laid the ground work so that I could get my degrees, get my business loans, as well as my mother who taught me the importance of education and that I could do anything if I put my mind to it.

But, I do think it has to be harder for us. I mean, I would love to have a "wife," and I know I am not the first to use this terminology. The 50's ideal of a wife to make a nice home, an oasis to relax from the office and take care of the kids would be great. It's a nice thought—until reality sets in—there's no way I could be that hands off. From that perspective, the thing I most envy about men is their ability to delegate and detach or to compartmentalize.

We are born multi-taskers—we keep the house together, the kids alive, and support our men historically. Men are hunter-gatherers—they focus to kill the prey for us to cook for the family. This is also why we are more social. We women stick together to help each other out—watch each other's children in an emergency, and give that cup of sugar to our neighbor.

Single. Women. Entrepreneurs.

A single man would have it easier as well because 1. We were raised to keep a home to a certain standard, usually, and 2. We have family and friends that expect to hear from us. My anecdotal experience in observing many men is that "bachelor" is more than being single, it's a way of keeping house, and keeping in touch with family and friends is a much lower priority or at least lower frequency than with women.

My mother and grandmother are both widowed. It's not a coincidence that they are part of the trend—women over 50 years of age are less likely to remarry. The usual reasons are that they do not want to: 1. Change their life or habits for another person again, and 2. Most of the men they meet are looking for a wife to "take care of" them.

What was the best training you received to prepare you as a business owner?

My various positions or work experience. They allowed me to learn how to do a lot of different things and they allowed me to see when management didn't do what it should have done. It inspired me to start my own business to call my own shots. After that, I'd say it was my first foray into self-employment as a contractor. That was where I started translating my work experience into business opportunities, and it's where I caught the entrepreneurial bug. Lastly, I'd say books and reading. Several books helped me learn and grow and build the skills I needed to succeed, including knowing when to let go of the ledge and jump into business.

Did you, or are you running your business as a part-time or full-time venture? Why?

I started part-time in 2002 after passing the Indiana Bar. When I returned to Indiana after my father died, I was not licensed to practice law in Indiana, so I accepted a senior management position in government. Government was my day job. I only had three clients from 2002 to 2005, when I decided to let go of the ledge and expand the practice to full-time. Ruby Law has been a full-time venture since January 2005. I do not believe that I could make Ruby Law succeed as a part-time business.

I personally feel that if your business is only part-time or you have to slow down your business to take a job to pay the bills, then you will not have the time to devote to your business to really nurture and grow it. Sometimes you need that "hunger" for money to light a fire under yourself to know you have the determination to make the business work. That being said, I started a seminar series called Finances 101 for Young Professionals in the fall of 2005. We will have our Seventh Annual Seminar Series next October. It has survived as an annual fall seminar series, and we are getting ready to set up a non-profit to further grow this non-profit business. However, it took us 3 years to find a regular venue and better format, 5 years to put up a website, 6 years to decide to create a real logo, and it does not provide income.

Determine your goals and the timeframe to reach them. If you want the business to support you financially as soon as possible, then you probably need to devote yourself to the business full-time. However, if your goals are more philanthropic or if you have other priorities or goals to reach first, then a part-time business may be the best route for you.

Did you take on a partner in your business at any time?

For Ruby Law, I still have not taken on a partner. I seriously thought about it and even who I would choose as a potential partner in my first year. But as I poured my blood, sweat and tears into my company, I had second thoughts. At this point, I am not sure that any amount of equity would be enough to allow someone else to claim partnership in my firm. Currently, I feel that I have worked too hard to share any of Ruby Law's "good will" with anyone.

However, Finances 101 for Young Professionals was born out of a networking conversation suggesting a concept for a seminar that would discuss finances from the perspective of an attorney, financial advisor and accountant. I needed a financial advisor and accountant to round out the seminar series. Therefore, I needed partners. I recruited the speakers, developed a plan for the series, obtained a venue, found sponsors, marketed the project and did the press releases. My husband still considers it to be my baby, but I just call myself the Founder. The accountant has been with the seminar series from the beginning, and the financial advisor has been with the seminar series since the second year. They are both Co-founders.

Although it began as a marketing tool, we learned in the first year that it would not yield clients. Young people just don't think they will die anytime soon. However, we feel strongly that Social Security will not be there for many of us, and that everyone needs some basic financial information to prepare for the future—whether or not they have the money to meet with attorneys, accountants or financial planners. I still do the lion's share of the work, but educating young people on financial issues is something that I am very passionate about.

If you had to start another business, what have you learned that you might do differently—either about yourself, or about how to run a business in general?
1. Plan every aspect of the business out before you have to rely on it financially,
2. Get all your tools in place before you open your doors,
3. Practice asking for money and be sure you can do it consistently and effectively,
4. Fund the business adequately (2-3 times) what you think you will need, and
5. Do your best to use other people's money.

Did you start your business with your own capital?
I started with my own capital, and continued to fund with a small business line of credit, equity line of credit, and credit cards. I do not recommend funding your business as I have done, but I know I am not the only person who has funded a business this way. However, I highly recommend building good business credit as soon as you can. I thought I was building my business credit with

my small business line of credit. I learned this spring that it didn't show up on any radar. At which point, I decided to lease the new office computer equipment instead of purchasing it and opened an American Express® Business Credit Card.

How important are your social and personal networks to the success of your business?

Essential. I earned the nickname "Princess of Networking" in my first 2 years of business, and I am still receiving the fruits of that labor. Networking must be part of your marketing and branding efforts, especially when you are a new business owner. You are your business.

Why do you think more single/divorced and widowed women start more businesses than men in their respective categories, and does your theory match your own rationale for starting a business?

I don't know for single women, but for divorced or widowed women it might be to regain control over their lives after a loss. Being a business owner can be very difficult at times, but the biggest payoff is to have more control over your own destiny—the ability to make time for your children and/or community and charitable interests.

The theory could be my rationale, but I had not thought about it in those terms. I had two failed relationships, a marriage and a live-in. Each time, I kept my career path moving forward, but I spent a great deal of time propping up the men in my life and helping them with their careers. I was trying to be their support—to hold them up and help them succeed. When my last relationship failed, for some reason, I felt deep down that a higher power was telling me that it was my turn to "be all that I could be" and my turn to "shine." In the end, the only person you control is yourself. You can't get anyone else a job or take a test for anyone else. No matter how much you want to help, you can't do it for them or ensure it will be done to your specifications.

Single. Women. Entrepreneurs.

What is your personal definition of success, and have you achieved it?

My philosophy is to live each day as if it were my last. I have a family, a thriving business, good friends, and I have been lucky enough to win accolades. I appreciate all that I have, so from this perspective, I feel that I am successful. BUT, as with most overachievers, I like challenges, so I am not "done" yet. I don't know that many people feel "done," if they want more out of life. There is always something else to do, some other challenge to undertake.

For me, my business is thriving, but I just started to turn a profit last year. I would like Ruby Law to be profitable enough to have several different locations in and around my city and maybe other states. Likewise, I would like Finances 101 for Young Professionals to be set up as a non-profit and financed to support a staff and a continuous stream of new projects and programs for financial literacy. I would like to have another child in the next year or two, and to put both of my children through their colleges of choice. I would like to make it to my 10-year wedding anniversary, renew our vows, throw a huge party and have a second honeymoon in Europe. I would like to have a business succession plan in place to turn over the day-to-day operations of my business to my children, or other worthy individual, to free up my time from client and administrative responsibilities. And, although I already donate time and money to charities, I would like to dramatically increase my ability to donate both.

What other single women business owners do you admire, and why?

All of them. Each and everyone who has put themselves out there and tried, succeeded or failed, they have all done so much more than so many. They are the largest growing segment of entrepreneurs and a beacon of determination, perseverance and possibilities.

Many women entrepreneurs are quietly doing great things. Most women are not good at tooting their own horns, so I probably don't know a lot of the most successful women entrepreneurs. We all need to be better at touting, not only our own successes, but also touting other women's successes. We need to be cheerleaders for each other, so that more and more women and young girls see the possibilities that life holds for them.

You started your business while you were single, but now you are married, you're running a business, and you have a child. What does the term "balance" mean to you, and have you found it?

If you are an entrepreneur, it's likely that you are an overachiever with control issues. The good news is that if you own your own business, you have more control over your schedule, which means you also have flexibility. That flexibility will allow you to accomplish your goals. I do not believe in "balance." In any given week, my needs, my family's needs, my client's needs, my business' needs, and my community needs are at different levels of highs and lows. You will frequently have many conflicting priorities, many in the same day or hour, all vying for your attention. How should you handle them?

First, make sure that you are following your values, mission & priorities. Sometimes it is helpful to draft a mission statement and list your priorities so that you, your family, your staff and your clients understand them. Understand that some shifting can occur based on time sensitive priorities or family or client emergencies, but what are the most important things for you to be doing?

- If the "to do" item doesn't fit within your values, mission or priorities, or it's not important, then eliminate it from your list. Learn to say NO. NO is a powerful tool in your arsenal.
- Next, scan for items that fit within your values, mission, and priorities, and see if any of them can have an acceptable shortcut, alternative solution, or can be postponed to another day or even week. Examples: The cupcakes or cookies for the girl or cub scouts are store

bought rather than homemade, likely the children won't care and your ego will only be slightly bruised. Dad or grandma may need to pick the kids up or run the errand rather than you. The laundry may wait another day for washing, and the dry cleaning may need to be picked up tomorrow, etc.
- Now, look at your list and prioritize it from most important to least.
- Lastly, start working your way through the list. If you can get easy items done while waiting for a call, on photocopies or whatever, go ahead squeeze those in.

Remember, being busy in business is almost always better than the alternative, and it will all get done.

Second, remember that you can't take care of anybody if you don't take care of yourself. The list doesn't leave much room for you. If you need to, steal the time from somewhere to take care of yourself. There are times when everything hits at once. If you can't eliminate anything, ride it out the best you can. But, definitely take time to recover when it's over. Children learn as much from what you say as what you do. Always remember that if you are good to yourself, your child will know how to be good to him or herself.

Third, make time for your spouse. You decided to marry the (wo)man and have children, so spend some time making sure that he or she remains a priority in your life. The marriage and that relationship must come before your kids, not the other way around. The relationship is why you have kids, and once the kids are grown and gone, the relationship is what will be left. You need to build a fun and fulfilling life together.

Fourth, kids don't need to do it all either. They need time to process what they've learned and to have relaxed fun. They also need you to spend some quality time with them. Quality time is when they know they are the only thing holding your attention—talking with or without a sit down meal, playing a game together, reading a book out loud together or working on a project indoors or out together. Watching TV or movies, or playing fast paced video games allows the activity to dominate the time, so these rarely count.

Fifth, don't compare and don't feel guilty. If you feel guilty, your priorities are probably out of whack. Refocus on what your priorities are. Let your husband and children know what your priorities are so they can help you keep on track and understand why you are saying no from time to time. But, don't compare with others—their priorities are not yours. Life is a journey, not a competition, so the important part is to be present in the moment and enjoy the ride.

What I Learned From This Project

This book is my sixth project. Each time I embark on a book journey, I learn something new. While I first hate to generalize and second do not like to stereotype, I'll begin this section with my usual disclaimer that while I received the following messages from this project below, others who read this book may have different messages. Bluntly, that's not only OK, but also GREAT! I want other people to get messages from books that are individualized. There's a great Buddhist proverb that states, "When the student is ready, the teacher will appear." So, I say, Y-A-Y if you found something different than I did as your own personal teacher.

Now, that aside, here is what I learned from these fabulous, bold, daring and amazing women:

- The biggest advantage to being a single woman entrepreneur is flexibility. The biggest disadvantage is not having a plan B, or significant other to share the joy of triumph and the agony of defeat. However, this can be overcome by having another good support system in friends and family.
- Business, personal and generalized coaching seems to help. In fact, I think I'm going to look into having a coach in my future!

- It isn't all about the money with women, and I believe I've confirmed from this research that women and men start businesses for different reasons. This could be a little overreaching; however, a lot of women interviewed for this project mentioned over and over again that starting a business wasn't really ONLY about the money. Yes, a sustainable living is nice, but most, if not all women in this book really want to truly make a difference in the lives of others through their businesses.

- Success and happiness are individualized. What you'll learn here that I didn't have in the interviews (but asked the women after their individual interviews) was whether or not they were happy. (Mind you, being "happy" is subjective, and different from being "successful.") Most women responded that overall, they were happy. There were a few exceptions to this, but I think the differences might have been based upon what profession they chose.

- Keep on learning. Nearly every woman discussed how important it is to keep understanding the developments of the industries they each chose, and to keep on improving their overall skills relative to entrepreneurship.

- One of the most interesting things I discovered during this project was that nearly 100% of the women I interviewed started their businesses with their own money. This begs the question—if venture capital out there is only going to the men in business, what would the world of business be like if women owned businesses were actually given a seat at the venture capital table? I think the world might be in a very different place, honestly. If you are a venture capitalist and reading this book, I invite you to please consider this.

- Running a business part-time vs. full-time is a personal choice. Furthermore, there appeared to be a theme of a "tipping point" or watershed moment for each woman who started her business part-time and then went on to running her business full-time. I'm going to stick my neck out here and say that running my businesses part-time, while holding down a day job has worked for me, at least thus far in my career. However, others feel as though if you don't focus on one thing, you might not be great at it. I'm going to take the road that I think this is a personal choice. Furthermore, I think smart women are going to start their businesses on a part-time basis and then grow them over time while holding down a day job. Because single women don't really have anyone else to fall back on, I think this is the more judicious approach to business. While others may disagree with me, that's fine, but especially with women using their own capital to start a business, women in my opinion would be wise to start a part-time business on top of a full-time day job.

- Relative to the last bullet, I also think the future of the employee or smart individual is going to demand that individuals do *more* than just one thing professionally. For example, we have more than a couple of women in this book who are moving multiple careers forward simultaneously. Again, I think this is a smart approach, and with the current horrific economic downturn that we are slowly crawling out from, I think we've received the message that industries can pretty much collapse overnight, which suggests that putting all your career eggs in only one basket is risky. The new "safe" actually is juggling multiple careers simultaneously. I might be wrong on this, but I think the evidence suggests otherwise.
- Network, find mentors, join groups, and get out of the office.
- Single women entrepreneurs are re-defining business. Some of the women (particularly the mompreneurs in this book) said they actually thought being a business owner was an *advantage* over working for corporate America. This should give the rest of us a lot of hope,

and it honestly was one of the biggest pleasant surprises I found while conducting this research. Besides, if you listen to all the gurus in business, microenterprise and small business will be where all the growth is in the U.S. in the future. If you're in city or state government, be sure that your city or state has fantastic, low cost resources for budding entrepreneurs to polish their skills. In Indianapolis, the Business Ownership Initiative of Indiana is a great example of this type of training and education a budding entrepreneurial culture needs.

- If you are a CEO of a big company in corporate America—please consider this book notice that your best and brightest might go elsewhere. I was a little alarmed that a lot of women in this book worked for corporate America and were just frustrated by the quashing of creativity and innovation. The good news for the best and brightest? See the previous bullet—small business owners will be driving the economic engine in the U.S. moving forward.

- If there was a way I could personally bottle the enthusiasm and passion the women in this book have for their businesses and sell it, I'd be a gazillionaire. Passion and enthusiasm, with a view on realism are the elements that people need to run a successful start up. However, I learned first hand after chasing down these rock star women that they are very BUSY. However, eventually, the women who wound up in this book were clearly passionate about their businesses, and in many if not all cases, happy and eager to help others get started in business.

I think as evidenced by the stories in this book, I am very encouraged to watch the changing face of business over the next few decades here in the U.S. A lot of women in this project remarked that the "old" way of doing business clearly wasn't working and caused the economic recession. I think they are on to something. Certainly, we don't want to forget the women who have gone before us, plowed some different paths and choices for us, and led us to the array of options we have today. Thanks be to them! (Including, but not limited to Jane Austen.) Last but not least, I can't wait to see where each of the 30 women in this book end up 10 years from now. It will be very exciting to watch!

Of course, the science geek in me always ends up with more questions after a research project than I started. This book was no exception. My major questions are after researching this book are—what about single men? What about married people and starting businesses? How are they the same? How are they different? *Are* they different? And what about the movement forward for a full time job and a part time business—will that be the new way of starting businesses moving forward and the 'safe' way to manage a career?

I don't know. But I certainly look forward to finding out!

Other Books
By The Author

Indianapolis: A Young Professional's Guide
Second Edition: AuthorHouse, 2010, ISBN: 978-1-4490-9530-7
First Edition: AuthorHouse, 2008, ISBN: 978-1-4343-6161-5

This is the definitive guide to the city of Indianapolis for the young professional—whether new to the city, moving to Indianapolis, or just trying to find better ways to connect to the city. Written by a young professional for other young professionals, the second edition of this guide not only includes over 40 categories of information for the young professional, but also includes 40 interviews with young professionals, or professionals who have "been there, and done that" relative to this great city.

The Life Science Lawyer
AuthorHouse, 2009, ISBN: 978-1-4389-1502-9

Healthcare and life sciences are increasingly complex. There are many global players in life sciences and healthcare—patients, governments, hospitals, managed care companies, pharmaceutical, biotechnology, and medical device companies and pharmacies are only a few. With the increasing complexity comes a higher demand for hybrid professionals who can translate both the science as well as the legal issues surrounding this complicated environment. This book compiles interviews and wisdom from over 30 hybrid law/ life science professionals, by a pre-1L dedicated to finding out what makes the life science lawyer tick.

Prescription To My Younger Self:
What I Learned After Pharmacy School

AuthorHouse, 2008, ISBN: 978-1-4343-6259-9

The current pharmacy doctorate curriculum is rigorous. Pharmacists must adopt a mantra of life long learning. In this book, students gave pharmacy leaders in academia, clinical practice, community practice, executive management, and government a simple assignment: write a letter to yourself from present day to yourself at graduation from pharmacy school, discussing the major lessons you learned after pharmacy school about yourself and your profession. Student authors/editors from Butler University College of Pharmacy & Health Sciences include: Alisha Broberg, Jennell Colwell, Brad Koselke, and Annah Steckel. Their project mentor at Butler was Dr. Erin Albert.

The Medical Science Liaison: An A to Z Guide

AuthorHouse, 2007, ISBN: 978-1-4343-3750-4

The medical science liaison (MSL) role was recently reported as one of the best jobs over six figures for healthcare professionals within the pharmaceutical industry, yet is relatively unknown, even to the medical community. What is a MSL, and what do they do? In this first, comprehensive, must-have guide to the role, the functions of the role of the MSL are explored, along with interviews with several MSLs, those who work around them, and most importantly, the customers of the MSL, academic thought leaders. Every healthcare professional, whether a pharmacist, a PhD or MD, should learn more about one of the greatest jobs that blend business, technical and scientific acumen.

For more information on the author,
visit www.erinalbert.com

By Erin Albert

Single. Women. Entrepreneurs.